JUNIOR DETECTIVE'S KIT
CONFIDENTIAL
STAY OUT!

Bruce Wayne
The young detective at work.

DC COMICS

SECRET HERO SOCIETY

STUDY HALL OF JUSTICE

Written by **Derek Fridolfs** | Illustrations by **Dustin Nguyen**

SCHOLASTIC INC.

To our editors; Rex, for helping launch us, and Michael, for seeing us through to the finish line.

To my teachers throughout the years who encouraged me to write inside and outside the margins.
To my parents, for their constant love and support.
And to Pamela, who listens to all my silly ideas with great enthusiasm. — Derek

Thanks to Mom, Phyllis, and my wife, Nicole, for always supporting my love for illustration, or at least putting up with it. — Dustin

ISBN 978-0-545-92907-3

10 9 8 7 6 5 4 3 2 1 16 17 18 19 20

PRINTED IN THE U.S.A. 23
FIRST PRINTING 2016

BOOK DESIGN BY RICK DEMONICO AND CHEUNG TAI

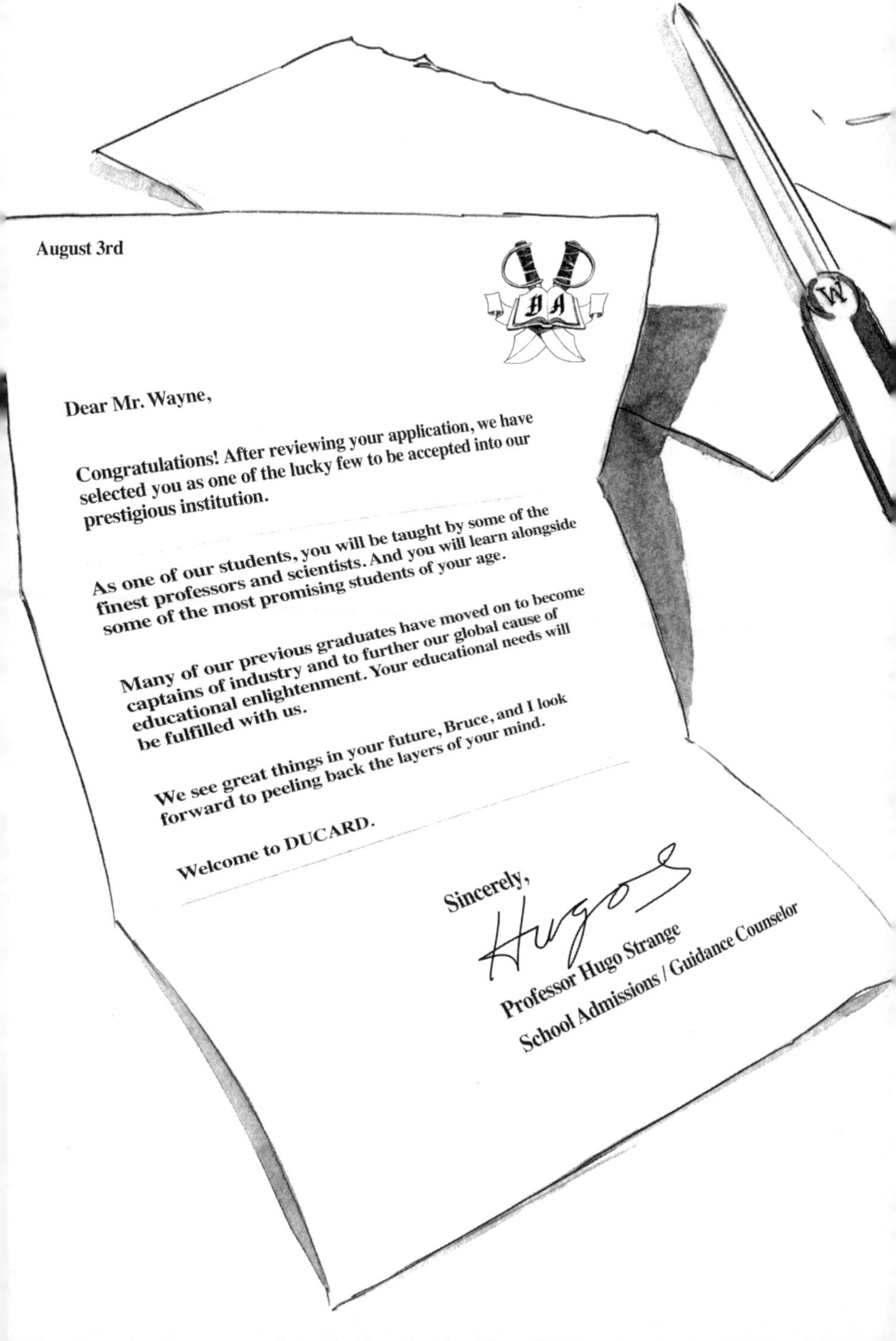

August 3rd

Dear Mr. Wayne,

Congratulations! After reviewing your application, we have selected you as one of the lucky few to be accepted into our prestigious institution.

As one of our students, you will be taught by some of the finest professors and scientists. And you will learn alongside some of the most promising students of your age.

Many of our previous graduates have moved on to become captains of industry and to further our global cause of educational enlightenment. Your educational needs will be fulfilled with us.

We see great things in your future, Bruce, and I look forward to peeling back the layers of your mind.

Welcome to DUCARD.

Sincerely,

Hugo

Professor Hugo Strange

School Admissions / Guidance Counselor

DATE: AUGUST 6

USERNAME: BWAYNE

RE: JOURNAL ENTRY 1

I JUST GOT MY ACCEPTANCE LETTER IN THE MAIL FOR THE DUCARD ACADEMY! ALFRED MADE ME WRITE SO MANY LETTERS TO EVERY SCHOOL THAT MY HAND ALMOST FELL OFF. BUT MY FIRST CHOICE ENDED UP BEING THE ONE I GOT, SO IT WAS A SUCCESS!

I CAN'T WAIT TO START AT MY NEW SCHOOL! NO MORE BORING TUTORS BROUGHT TO THE MANSION, OR ALFRED'S "ETIQUETTE" LESSONS. AND THE BEST PART—NO MORE CHORES! BUT ALFRED PROMISES ME MY CHORES WILL BE WAITING FOR ME WHEN I GET HOME FROM SCHOOL EACH DAY. *NOT FAIR!!*

I HOPE THE CAFETERIA FOOD IS AS GOOD AS ALFRED'S COOKING. DON'T TELL HIM I SAID THAT OR HE'LL ASK FOR A RAISE!

THE DUCARD ACADEMY
SCHOOL ORIENTATION
WELCOME NEW STUDENTS AND PROSPECTIVE CONQUERORS OF TOMORROW!
• Meet the administration staff
• Meet the teachers and current students
• Supervised tour of the school grounds . . . Please stay with your group
• Campus map and class schedule handout
• Sports and extracurricular preregistration
• School uniform fitting and pickup

ORIENTATION DAY
YOU ARE HERE FOR THE TOUR. I WILL SHOW YOU.
NOW. SINGLE FILE.

HMMF. . . FOLLOW ME BUT DO NOT STRAY.
TOUR IS OVER! EVERYONE REPORT TO SCHOOL TOMORROW.
THAT IS ALL.

DATE: AUGUST 14

USERNAME: BWAYNE

RE: JOURNAL ENTRY 2

NOTES: ORIENTATION WASN'T WHAT I WAS EXPECTING. IT GAVE ME A BAD FEELING, BUT MAYBE IT'S JUST NEW-SCHOOL JITTERS. STILL, IT WOULDN'T HURT TO RESEARCH THE SCHOOL ON MY OWN. HERE ARE MY RESULTS . . .

SYSTEMS CHECK = [Y/N]

ENTER COMMAND = HISTORY OF THE DUCARD ACADEMY

PROCEEDING . . .

SCHOOL FOUNDER —> ACCESS DENIED

CREST HISTORY —> ACCESS DENIED

STAFF BACKGROUND —> ACCESS DENIED

CRIMINAL HISTORY —> ? // FILE NOT FOUND

ENROLLMENT —> ACCESS DENIED

PARENTAL COMPLAINTS —> 0

RESULTS —> INCONCLUSIVE

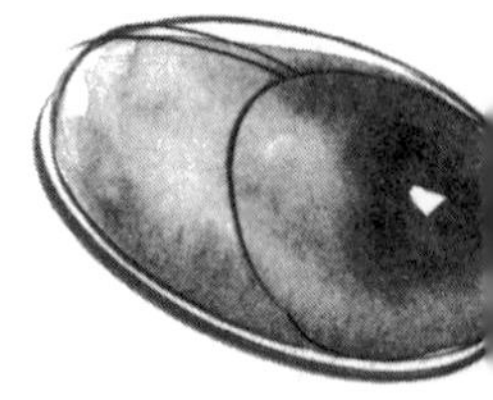

PRINCIPAL
HOW DO THE NEW STUDENTS LOOK?
THE RECRUITS?
"STUDENTS"! WE MUST KEEP UP APPEARANCES.
THEY ARE YOUNG. EAGER. MAYBE TOO EAGER.
THERE'S ONE . . . THE RICH KID . . . VERY NOSY. HE COULD BE TROUBLE FOR US.
I'LL BE SURE TO KEEP AN EYE ON HIM. I'VE ALREADY STARTED.

WHAT TO BRING . . .

- ❑ Enrollment letter
- ❑ Application
- ❑ Photo ID (Secret identities need not apply) Wait—WHAT?!
- ❑ Medical history
- ❑ Pen and paper
- ❑ Absolute loyalty That's kinda weird.

WHAT NOT TO BRING . . .

- ❑ Parents
- ❑ Adults Looks like you're staying home, Alfred.
- ❑ Authorities Hmm . . .

WHAT I NEED TO BRING (ALFRED'S SHOPPING LIST)

Infrared and night vision goggles

Military-grade stealth suit with grappling hook

Portable chem lab for analyzing microfragments and fingerprints

Computer with advanced facial recognition software

Pudding cups (chocolate peanut butter)

I am NOT buying you any of this! But I will buy you new underwear.
—Alfred

SEPTEMBER 1—FIRST DAY OF SCHOOL

FORGETTING SOMETHING, MASTER BRUCE?
ALFRED, QUIT IT! EVERYONE IS STARING.
ALL THE MORE REASON TO LOOK PRESENTABLE.
YOU ARE A REFLECTION ON ME, EVEN IF YOU ARE GRUMPY.
I HAVE ALSO PREPARED YOUR LUNCH. GRANOLA . . . VERY HEALTHY.

Activate motion detectors
Install hidden camera and recording device here
Remove panel for secret compartment
The Man Who Laughs -Hugo
Detective Handbook
SHARK REPELLENT
-menu-
Mystery Meat Monday
Taco Tuesday
Chicken Wing Wednesday
Tater Tot Thursday
French Fry day

HEY, I'M TALKING TO YOU, FOUR-EYES!
HOW MANY FISTS AM I HOLDING UP? HERE, LET ME SHOW YOU!
HEY, YOU GUYS, LEAVE THAT KID ALONE.
WHERE DO YOU THINK YOU'RE GOING?
GET A LOAD OF HIS SILLY CLOTHES!
IT'S OUR SCHOOL UNIFORM. EVERYONE IS SUPPOSED TO WEAR THEM.
BUT WHEN YOU WEAR IT, IT LOOKS ***LAME***.
LET ME GUESS. I'M THE NEW KID. THIS IS WHERE YOU THREATEN ME FOR MY LUNCH MONEY. RIGHT?

SPLAT!
WRONG!
WHO WANTS MONEY? LAUGHS ARE WORTH MORE.
TEE-HEE! GOOD ONE, PUDDIN'.
SEE YA LATER, NEWBIE. HELLO AND GOOD-BYE!
NOPE . . . GOOD PIE! HEE-HEE-HEEEE!
BOYS
IT'S SAFER TO JUST KEEP TO MYSELF.
WISH THEY'D TAKEN MY MONEY INSTEAD.

IT TOOK ME THREE HOURS TO PREPARE THAT. YOU NEED TO EAT YOUR DINNER.
I'M NOT HUNGRY.
I'VE DECIDED I DON'T LIKE THIS SCHOOL.
YOU'RE NOT SUPPOSED TO . . . IT'S SCHOOL.
THAT'S NOT WHAT I MEANT. SOMETHING FEELS OFF.
IT WAS YOUR FIRST DAY. IT WILL GET BETTER. YOU NEED TO STICK THIS OUT.
I *ORDER* YOU TO MAKE THIS WORK!
ORDER, LIKE A MISSION . . . A DETECTIVE'S MISSION . . .
A CASE!

DATE: SEPTEMBER 1

USERNAME: BWAYNE

RE: JOURNAL ENTRY 3

MY FIRST DAY AT SCHOOL WASN'T WHAT I WAS EXPECTING. IT'S SUPPOSED TO BE THE BEST ACADEMY FOR LEARNING IN GOTHAM CITY. BUT THE ONLY THING I LEARNED IS THAT NO SCHOOL IS PERFECT.

AM I JUST LOOKING FOR THE WORST, LIKE ALFRED SAYS?

ALFRED THINKS I'M A SCARED LITTLE BOY WHO NEEDS TO LEARN TO FOLLOW THE RULES. BUT I MUST GET TO THE BOTTOM OF WHAT'S GOING ON AT DUCARD.

YOU DON'T LOOK FAMILIAR.
MR. GRUNDY
BRUCE WAYNE.
I HATE MONDAYS . . .
TODAY IS TUESDAY.
GRRR . . . TAKE SEAT.

HI!
YOU CAN SIT WITH US, IF YOU WANT.
WAS IT SOMETHING I SAID?

THE FACULTY

PRINCIPAL

PROFESSOR HUGO STRANGE
(School Admissions / Guidance Counselor)

DR. THADDEUS B. SIVANA
(Science)

MR. VANDAL SAVAGE
(History)

MR. JERVIS TETCH
(Literature)

MR. BASIL KARLO
(Theater/Arts)

MS. SIOBHAN McDOUGAL
(Choir)

COACH ZOD
(Boys' Physical Ed.)

COACH "KITTY" FAULKNER
(Girls' Physical Ed.)

MR. SOLOMON GRUNDY
(Homeroom)

HISTORY CLASS
"THE HISTORY OF MAN"
TEACHER—MR. VANDAL SAVAGE

COURSE DESCRIPTION:

To examine the nature of humankind throughout history, from the dawn of civilization to the present.

COURSE OBJECTIVES:

To give an introduction to the origin and development of humankind throughout the ages. Our greatest successes, our failures, our inventions, discoveries, and impulses. To talk about human achievement in construction, science, technology, military, and politics. To discuss where we've been as a species and where we're going. These and other topics will provide lectures and group discussion, and be examined through quizzes and testing.

drawings elicit a positive response by teacher, who is made fun of.
useful evidence to keep a file on him

THE REST OF YOU WILL LEARN HISTORY. BUT THIS CLASS CLOWN *IS* HISTORY.
REPORT TO DETENTION.

HISTORY 101

All great empires reach a pinnacle of distinction and achievement before their inevitable destruction. Some due to the rise in power of their enemies. Some due to their own shortcomings. History is built on the rise and fall of these great empires and civilizations. But everything you've read is what they've chosen to tell you. And it has been wrong. No matter how bright the success, it is the shadows cast from their brilliance that are there to direct the course of the future.

What does this hold for your future?

Look to the Shadows . . .

Photo Evidence
—September 4
No one can run this fast. Remember to reinforce my locker for safety!
This isn't a clown school . . . Why is he here?
Is this girl flying? Not possible!
Ninja here
Ninja
Also here

DATE: SEPTEMBER 4

USERNAME: BWAYNE

RE: JOURNAL ENTRY 4

THIS SCHOOL IS WEIRD!

YESTERDAY I FELT A KID BLUR PAST ME. TODAY I WITNESSED A GIRL FLYING THROUGH THE AIR. I'M NOT KIDDING. NOT TO MENTION THERE'S A TON OF CLOWNS AND . . . I THINK I'VE EVEN SEEN NINJA LURKING ABOUT.

IT'S CRAZY.

MY MIND AND BODY HAVE BEEN TRAINED BY THE VERY BEST (ALFRED SAW TO THAT WITH PRIVATE TUTORS). MY EYES AREN'T PLAYING TRICKS. SO THERE MUST BE A LOGICAL EXPLANATION FOR IT.

MY INVESTIGATION CONTINUES. BUT I MUST ALSO MAKE TIME TO BEAT LEVEL SEVEN OF ***VIGILANTE FIGHTER TURBO***. RESIST THE URGE TO DOWNLOAD A CHEAT CODE.

I have made your favorite sandwich—
peanut butter and banana. You will notice
I have removed the crust from the bread,
as per your request. You are welcome.

Please do have a productive day at
school. If you are not there to get a better
education, then at least make use of your
time in other ways that are constructive.
Make friends. Take part in activities.
Have that thing that the children call . . .
what is it . . . oh, yes . . . "FUN"!

—Alfred

SEPTEMBER 5 . . .
HIGH IQ'S ONLY! YOU DON'T BELONG.
GET LOST!
YOOO-HOOO . . . OVER HERE. JOIN US FOR A LAUGH, BRUCIE!

WHAT'RE YOU EATING?
PEANUT BUTTER AND BANANA. MY BUTLER PACKED IT.
I PICKED MINE MYSELF. WE GROW EVERYTHING FRESH ON THE FARM.
I MEAN, ER, THE FOOD WAS DELIVERED HERE. YEAH.
GREEK FOOD FOR ME. STUFFED GRAPE LEAVES. WANT TO TRY?
EW! NO WAY!
I MEAN . . . NO THANKS.

DATE: SEPTEMBER 5

USERNAME: BWAYNE

RE: JOURNAL ENTRY 5

SCHOOL IS FILLED WITH ALL KINDS OF KIDS. NERDS, JOCKS, CHEERLEADERS, AND CLASS CLOWNS. THEY'RE HARD TO AVOID.

I HAVE STARTED TO EAT IN THE LIBRARY INSTEAD AND MET OTHERS LIKE ME. CLARK IS A FARM KID FROM SMALLVILLE. DIANA IS AN EXCHANGE STUDENT FROM ACROSS THE SEA. THEY BOTH LIVE IN THE DORMS, AND THEY'RE IN MY HOMEROOM, TOO.

AT FIRST I THOUGHT THEY WERE ANNOYING. BUT THEY'RE AS CONFUSED AS I AM ABOUT SCHOOL. THEY ALSO WERE EXCITED ABOUT COMING HERE UNTIL THEY HAD THE SAME PROBLEMS.

MAYBE I DON'T HAVE TO INVESTIGATE THIS SCHOOL ALONE. MAYBE WE CAN DO IT TOGETHER. IT'S SOMETHING WORTH CONSIDERING.

SEPTEMBER 8—FIELD NOTES

It's the start of my second week at DUCARD and my experience hasn't improved.

Theater class this morning with Mr. Basil Karlo was weird. His room was filled with nothing but old posters of the movies he's been in. I think playing a "teacher" is his current act, because he stole a kid's backpack right in front of him—as part of the lesson! He told us to act like the people we want to become and take what we want. What kind of a class is this?!

Also I think he was sweating mud. SERIOUSLY!! I managed to take a sample of the claylike substance. Will run tests on it later. This school . . . this world . . . is bigger and weirder than I thought.

SCHOOL ANNOUNCEMENTS

- **Boys' sports:**

All pain, some gain!
To sign up, see Coach Zod

- **Cheer squad tryouts**

Friday, October 10 at 3:00 p.m. after school
in the girls' gymnasium

- **JOIN the bird-watchers society!**

If interested, see club president
Oswald Cobblepot.

- **NEED a tutor?**

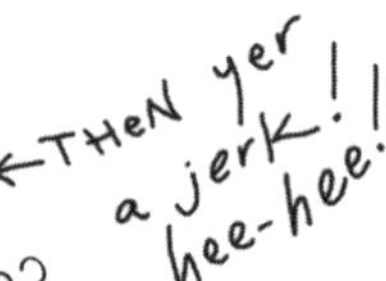

Inspired by world domination?
Evil geniuses wanted.

STOP EATING! THIS IS IMPORTANT!
BRUCE, WHAT'S WRONG?
THIS!
SCHOOL ANNOUNCEMENTS
Boys' sports:
All pain, some gain!
To sign up, see Coach Zod
SO . . . ARE YOU INTERESTED IN BIRD-WATCHING?
WHAT?! NO! NOT THAT!
DON'T YOU SEE IT?! IT'S RIGHT IN FRONT OF YOU.

I AM BRAINIAC,
THE AUTOMATED OPERATING SYSTEM FOR DUCARD.
ARE YOU HERE TO ANSWER THE AD FOR WORLD DOMINATION?
NO, WE'RE NOT!
PITY!
RETURN ALL OVERDUE BOOKS AND PERSONAL DATA IMMEDIATELY.
SEEEE?
THAT WAS STRANGE.
DEFINITELY STRANGE!
AND THERE ARE MORE WEIRD THINGS HAPPENING AROUND HERE, TOO.
I'M LATE FOR CLASS. WE'LL TALK MORE LATER.

DIANA'S DIARY
SEPTEMBER 10

Ever since that weird computer talked to us in the library, I've been on edge. Bruce is right! There are a lot of strange things happening around here. It's a shame because this school seemed so promising in their invite letter. I was so excited to enroll and now all I am is mad. I've broken six pencils trying to write it all down.

Like, I just got out of literature class, and I'm starting to notice more things. Our teacher, Mr. Tetch, is forcing us to read only one book in class: *Alice's Adventures in Wonderland*. I mean, that book's okay. But the only one we're going to read? And that's not the only weird thing. He keeps a pet bunny that hops around the classroom. He calls every girl Alice (EVEN ME)! And he dresses just like the Mad Hatter. He gives me the creeps!

SCHOOL NURSE INCIDENT REPORT

STUDENT: Clark Kent

TEACHER: Ms. Siobhan McDougal

CLASS: Choir

DATE: September 10

DESCRIPTION OF THE INCIDENT:

Choir class today was described as being extra rowdy. When Ms. McDougal couldn't get control over her students, it was reported that she screamed. The volume of her voice was so loud, it broke the windows, and many students' ears were ringing.

ACTION TAKEN:

Most students were administered cotton and gauze to prevent swelling and provide protection. Any who felt dizzy were sent home.

FURTHER RECOMMENDED CARE:

None. Clark is one of the few that appears unaffected. He seems to have exhibited extraordinary hearing and durability. No further action is to be taken.

NOTES:

He possesses remarkable strength for his age. Perhaps he is extraordinary in other ways, too.

IF YOU HAVE ANY QUESTIONS ABOUT THIS EVENT, PLEASE CALL THE NURSE'S OFFICE.

HAVE YOU NOTICED NO ONE IS EVER IN HERE STUDYING?
IT'S BECAUSE NO ONE IS HERE TO LEARN.
THAT JOKER IS IN HOME EC MAKING PIES TO THROW AT PEOPLE. BANE SPENDS ALL DAY IN THE GYM LIFTING WEIGHTS.
DON'T GET ME STARTED ON LITERATURE CLASS.
OR CHOIR.
YOU SING? *AWW*, THAT'S SWEET.

THIS SCHOOL IS WAY WORSE THAN THE LAST ONE I WAS IN.
WHY'D YOU LEAVE THE LAST ONE?
THEY HAD A CROOKED CANDY FUND-RAISER. *VERY* CROOKED.
NEVER MIND THAT! IF I TRANSFER AGAIN, I MIGHT END UP GOING TO A BOARDING SCHOOL IN ENGLAND. AND I HATE TEA. ***HATE!***
BUT SOMETHING IS REALLY WRONG WITH THIS SCHOOL, AND I PLAN ON FINDING OUT, NO MATTER WHAT IT TAKES.
WHAT DO YOU HAVE IN MIND?
I WANT TO FORM A SECRET GROUP TO INVESTIGATE.
LIKE A JUNIOR DETECTIVES' CLUB!
NO, NOT LIKE THAT . . . THAT'S FOR LITTLE KIDS.
DO YOU HAVE ANY IMPORTANT DATA YOU WISH TO SHARE?
NO!
MEET BACK HERE FRIDAY AFTER SCHOOL. THEN WE CAN DISCUSS IT MORE . . . PRIVATELY.

DUE TO THE KANDOR VIRUS

THE SCHOOL LIBRARY WILL BE CLOSED
ON FRIDAY, SEPTEMBER 12,
FOR COMPUTER MAINTENANCE,
NETWORK RECONFIGURATION, AND
THE RECOVERY OF LOST DATA.

BRAINIAC IS SORRY
FOR THIS INCONVENIENCE
AND VOWS REVENGE.

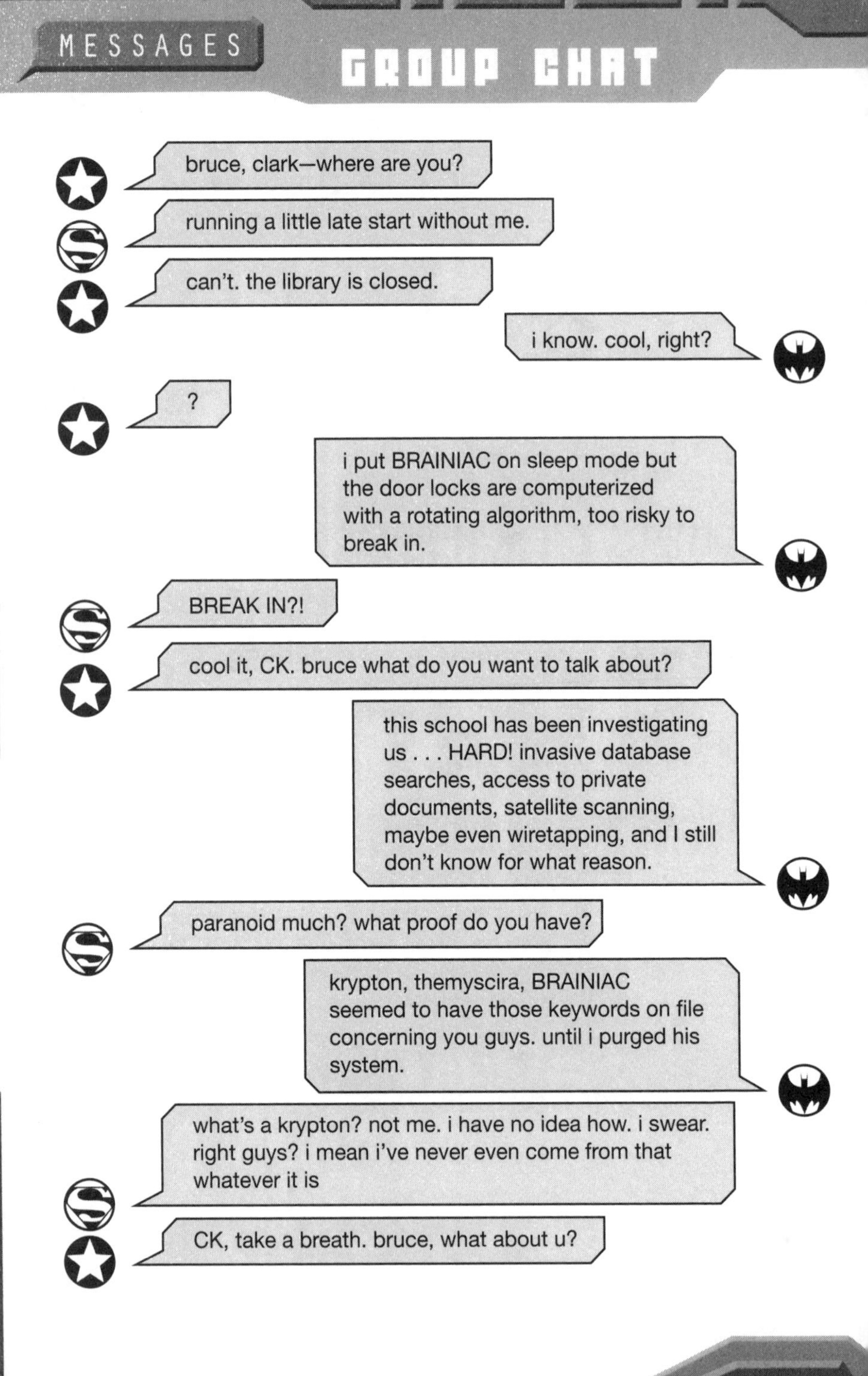
MESSAGES
GROUP CHAT
bruce, clark—where are you?
running a little late start without me.
can't. the library is closed.
i know. cool, right?
?
i put BRAINIAC on sleep mode but the door locks are computerized with a rotating algorithm, too risky to break in.
BREAK IN?!
cool it, CK. bruce what do you want to talk about?
this school has been investigating us . . . HARD! invasive database searches, access to private documents, satellite scanning, maybe even wiretapping, and I still don't know for what reason.
paranoid much? what proof do you have?
krypton, themyscira, BRAINIAC seemed to have those keywords on file concerning you guys. until i purged his system.
what's a krypton? not me. i have no idea how. i swear. right guys? i mean i've never even come from that whatever it is
CK, take a breath. bruce, what about u?
SEND

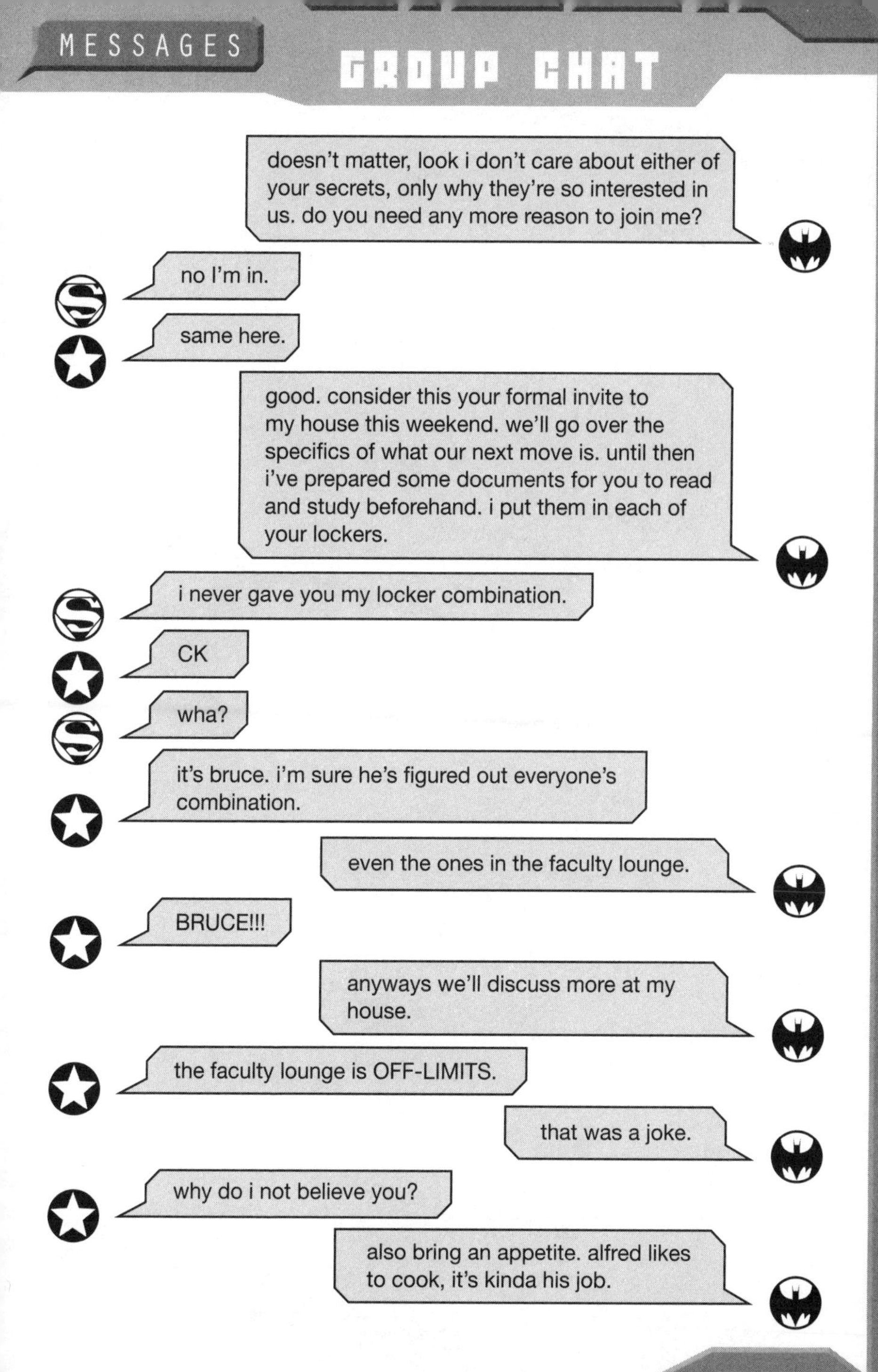
MESSAGES
GROUP CHAT
doesn't matter, look i don't care about either of your secrets, only why they're so interested in us. do you need any more reason to join me?
no I'm in.
same here.
good. consider this your formal invite to my house this weekend. we'll go over the specifics of what our next move is. until then i've prepared some documents for you to read and study beforehand. i put them in each of your lockers.
i never gave you my locker combination.
CK
wha?
it's bruce. i'm sure he's figured out everyone's combination.
even the ones in the faculty lounge.
BRUCE!!!
anyways we'll discuss more at my house.
the faculty lounge is OFF-LIMITS.
that was a joke.
why do i not believe you?
also bring an appetite. alfred likes to cook, it's kinda his job.
SEND

SEPTEMBER 12—FIELD NOTES

HOW TO BE A GOOD INVESTIGATOR
BY BRUCE WAYNE

- Be observant and aware of your surroundings. Evidence is everywhere.
- Look at everything and underneath everything.
- Find the answers with your eyes. Use your fists as a last resort.
- Spot clues.
- Have your tools handy.
- Read lots of mystery books.
- Research, research, research!
- Be safe, not reckless.

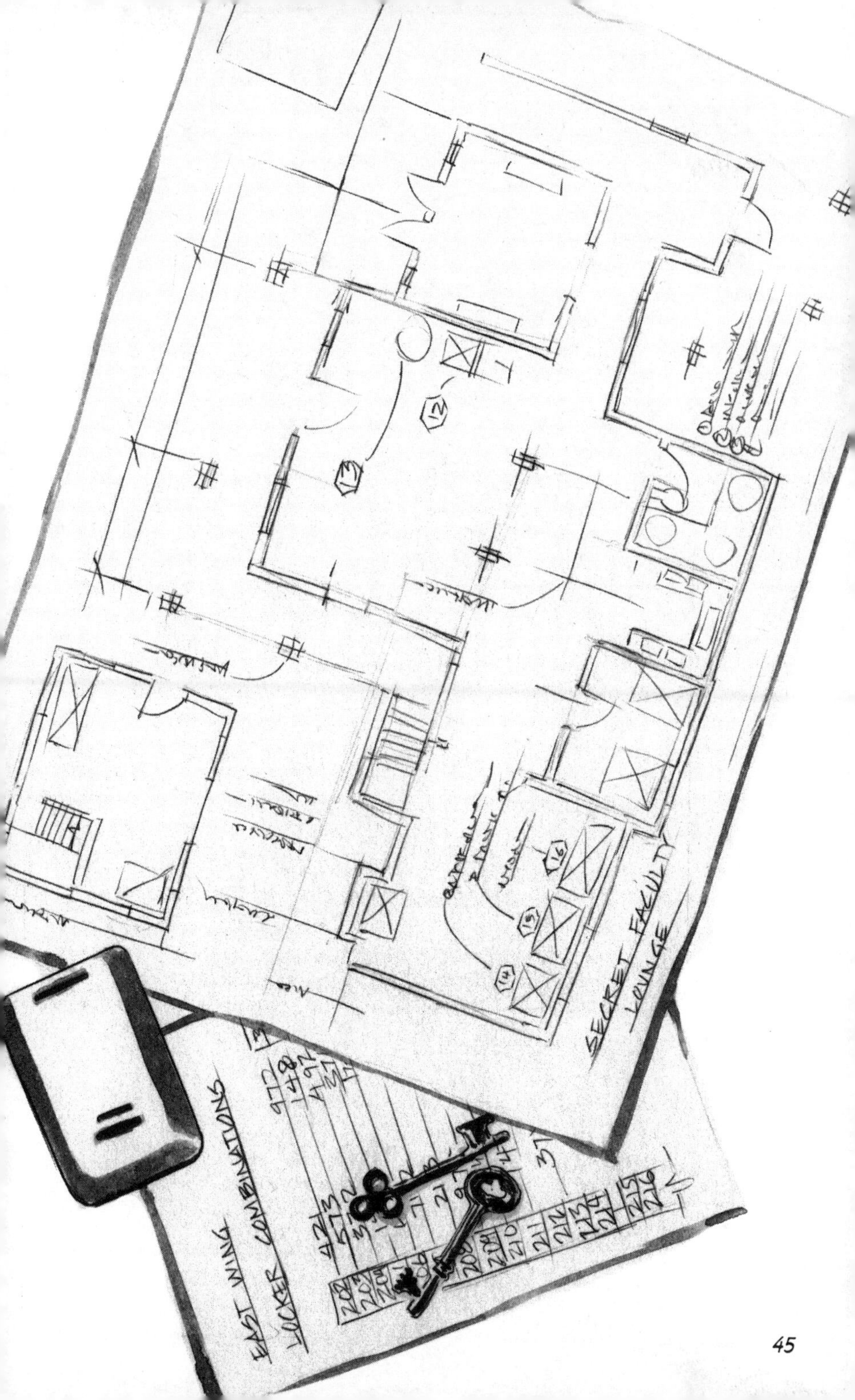
SECRET FACULTY LOUNGE
EAST WING
LOCKER COMBINATIONS

WEST PATHWAY
UNIT 7
UNIT 8
UNIT 9
UNIT 10
HVAC

THAT WEEKEND . . .
THIS IS SO MUCH FUN. I USUALLY JUST FLY WHERE I WANT TO GO.
HEY, ME, TOO!
HEY, GUYS! THIS IS MY HOUSE.
MORE LIKE A MANSION.
IT'S HOME.
YOU MUST REALLY LIKE BATS. THERE'S A CAVE UNDER YOUR MANSION.
HOW DID YOU KNOW THAT?!
I CAN'T SEE THROUGH WALLS OR ANYTHING. JUST A GUESS.

WELCOME TO THE FIRST MEETING OF THE CIU.
CRIMINAL INVESTIGATION UNIT.

A "JUNIOR DETECTIVES' CLUB" . . . HOW SPLENDID!
ALFRED! THAT'S SOMETHING A KID WOULD CALL IT.
WHICH YOU ALL CERTAINLY ARE NOT!
YOU'LL EXCUSE ME; I'LL MAKE LUNCH FOR YOU "INVESTIGATORS."

SEPTEMBER 30—FIELD NOTES

MISSION #1—INFILTRATION

Our priority is for each of us to infiltrate various sectors of school and report back our findings.

BRUCE: I will attempt to "make friends" as a way to get information.

CLARK: You've been tasked with becoming "hall monitor." From that position, you'll be able to view any suspicious activity without drawing any attention.

DIANA: Your task is to join the cheer squad. It can provide different clues and leads to check up on.

We'll meet back in the library at the end of school each day to report our findings.

CAFETERIA-MONITOR 02
12:51:05
LIBRARY-MONITOR 03
02:25:16
CAFETERIA-MONITOR 04
12:36:19

DATE: OCTOBER 1

USERNAME: BWAYNE

RE: JOURNAL ENTRY 6

SO I TRIED TO MAKE FRIENDS TODAY. THAT DIDN'T GO SO WELL.

FIRST I DEVELOPED A DISGUISE SO I WOULDN'T BE RECOGNIZED. I CREATED "MATCHES MALONE," A ROUGH KID FROM ACROSS THE TRACKS, WITH HELP FROM A COSTUME AND MAKEUP I FOUND IN THEATER CLASS. BUT MY DISGUISE WAS BLOWN WHEN THE DRAMA TEACHER ANNOUNCED IT TO THE SCHOOL. THE TEACHERS ARE JUST AS BAD AS THE STUDENTS!

THE JOCKS ONLY WANTED TO USE ME AS TARGET PRACTICE. EVERY BALL IN GYM HAS NOW HIT ME. WORSE, THEY DUMPED ME IN THE TRASH. BANE EVEN TRIED TO PUT ME IN A WRESTLING HOLD, BUT I MANAGED TO GET AWAY.

THE NERDS HAD ALREADY MADE UP THEIR MINDS THAT I WASN'T SMART ENOUGH FOR THEM. THEY SHOWED ME EVERY REPORT CARD I'VE EVER GOTTEN AND EVERY TEST SCORE I'VE RECEIVED, AND LAUGHED AT ME. HOW DO THEY HAVE ACCESS TO THAT?! BESIDES, EVERYONE KNOWS I'M A GENIUS. IT'S JUST A FACT.

THE CLOWNS WERE THE ONLY ONES WILLING TO GIVE ME A SHOT. BUT THE JOKE WAS ENTIRELY ON ME, SINCE THEY SET ME UP. THE FOOD FIGHT I WAS ASKED TO START WAS TURNED AROUND ON ME AND THE ENTIRE SCHOOL JOINED IN . . . EVEN THE LUNCH LADY. I STILL SMELL LIKE FRENCH FRIES.

BEING REJECTED BY EVERYONE IS DEPRESSING. BUT I HAVE TO REMEMBER NOT TO TAKE IT PERSONALLY. I REALLY DON'T WANT ANY OF THESE STUDENTS AS MY FRIENDS. I'M ONLY DOING IT TO GET INFORMATION.

HALLWAY-MONITOR 01
10:06:23

FOUNTAIN-MONITOR 02
10:07:14

HALLWAY-MONITOR 03
10:11:44

HALLWAY-MONITOR 03
10:15:06

HALLWAY-MONITOR 03
10:15:08

HALLWAY-MONITOR 03
10:15:11

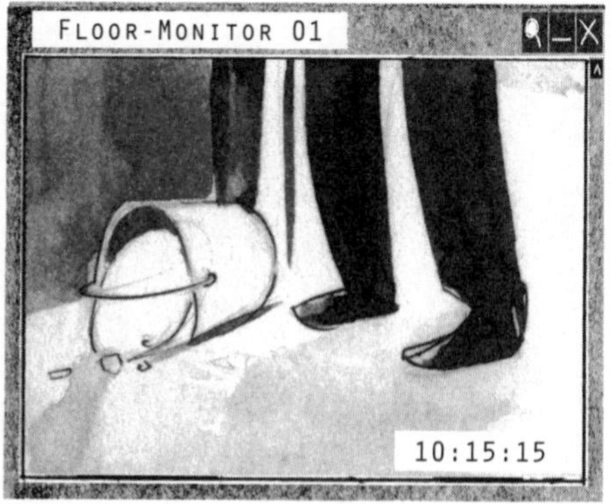
FLOOR-MONITOR 01
10:15:15

HALLWAY-MONITOR 02
HALL MONITOR
10:15:48

OFFICE-MONITOR 01
10:16:34

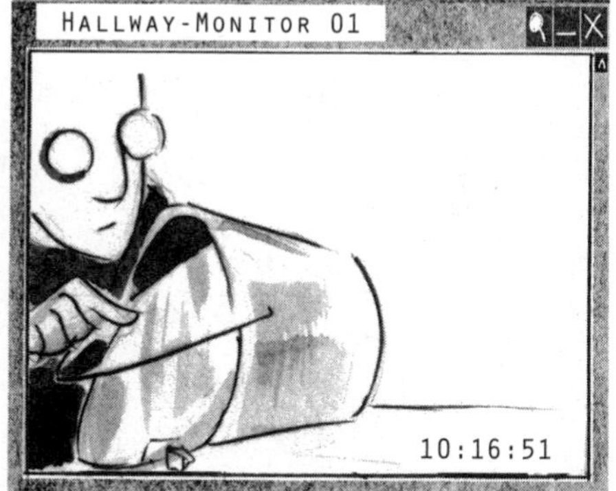
HALLWAY-MONITOR 01
10:16:51

HALL MONITOR—INCIDENT REPORT

STUDENT: JOE KERR

DATE: OCTOBER 7

LOCATION: BOYS' BATHROOM / HALL

INCIDENT:

Subject was caught with friends trying to prank another student with a bucket of water. He was apprehended before he could finish the act.

ADDITIONAL NOTES:

This student and his friends have repeatedly been found without hall passes, have been caught loitering, and committing general acts of delinquency.

MONITOR ON DUTY: CLARK KENT

Report never got a response and was dismissed. I fished it from the office trash to keep on file for my own records.

—B

YOU CALLED FOR ME?
INDEED.
I'VE BEEN FOLLOWING THE MONITORS AND READING THE REPORTS. WHILE MOST OF OUR STUDENT PROSPECTS APPEAR TO BE ACCLIMATING WELL, THERE ARE A FEW THAT AREN'T.
I WANT YOU TO EVALUATE THEM . . . SEPARATELY. GET INSIDE THEIR HEADS. FIND OUT MORE ABOUT THEM.
I'LL EXPECT REPORTS ON MY DESK SOON.
AS YOU WISH.

DA
DUCARD ACADEMY
CHEER SQUAD TRYOUTS
Cheer your team to battle!
Chant your battle cry!
Conquer your enemies!
Dance in their defeat!
FRIDAY, OCTOBER 10–3:00 p.m.
Grass field behind the girls' gymnasium

OSWALD PASSED YOU A NOTE IN CLASS, CIRCE?
HE'S SUCH A SILLY BIRD.
UM . . . EXCUSE ME?
YES, *EXCUSE YOU!*
I'M HERE FOR THE TRYOUTS?
FINE. SHOW US A CHEER.
WE'VE GOT TRUTH! WE'VE GOT PRIDE! WE'VE GOT JUSTICE ON OUR SIDE. WE WILL NOT BE DENIED. EVIL RUNS, BUT CANNOT HIDE.
2-4-6-8 PEACE, LOVE, AND NEVER HATE . . .

OKAY, OKAY, WE'VE HEARD ENOUGH. SHEESH!
READY TO VOTE, GIRLS?
WE'VE GOT SPIRIT, YES, WE DO!
YOU'VE GOT NO SPIRIT . . . AND PEEEE YEEEWWW!
HA-HA-HA-HA!
KRAK!
HEY! WHO DID THIS? THE GRASS DIDN'T DESERVE THAT!

DATE: OCTOBER 10

USERNAME: BWAYNE

RE: JOURNAL ENTRY 7

I'M DISAPPOINTED THAT OUR FIRST MISSIONS HAVE BEEN A DISASTER.

AS HALL MONITOR, CLARK SPENT MORE TIME WRITING REPORTS THAN FINDING OUT ANYTHING USEFUL. SO I TOLD HIM TO JOIN THE SCHOOL NEWSPAPER. THAT WAY HE CAN WRITE AS MUCH AS HE WANTS AND EXPOSE ANYTHING ODD.

DIANA DIDN'T DO SO HOT, EITHER. SHE DIDN'T FIT IN WITH THE GIRLS ON THE CHEER SQUAD. THEY VIEWED HER AS AN OUTSIDER. AND WORSE . . . NOT COOL.

I SUGGESTED HER NEXT MISSION COULD BE ONE OF DIPLOMACY. BUT SHE GROWLED AT ME AND SAID SHE'D TAKE ATHLETICS INSTEAD. PUNCHING MY LOCKER WAS HER WAY OF ENDING OUR TALK DIPLOMATICALLY.

I WILL KEEP FINDING OTHER WAYS TO INVESTIGATE. BUT FIRST I HAVE A “MANDATORY ASSESSMENT” MEETING WITH THE GUIDANCE COUNSELOR. THIS MIGHT COME IN HANDY, SINCE PROFESSOR HUGO STRANGE EVALUATES ALL STUDENTS AT DUCARD.

STUDENT EVALUATION REPORT

STUDENT: Bruce Wayne **PROFESSOR:** Hugo Strange

Which of the following best describes you?
Choose only one:

❑ Ambitious ❑ Angry ❑ Bored ❑ Calm ❑ Confused ❑ Creative ❑ Embarrassed
❑ Excited ☒ Focused ❑ Happy ❑ Hungry ❑ Lonely ❑ Loved ❑ Patient
❑ Proud ❑ Relieved ❑ Sad ❑ Scared ❑ Surprised ❑ Tired ❑ Other

Please rate the following based on how you are feeling about each area of your life:

Friendships
Terrible — Great
1 2 3 4 (5) 6 7 8 9 10

Home/Family
Terrible — Great
1 2 3 4 (5) 6 7 8 9 10

Grades/School
Terrible — Great
1 2 3 4 (5) 6 7 8 9 10

Diagnosis:
My assessment is that Bruce lives a very private life. Not willing to open up or give clues to what he's thinking. He answered all my questions very carefully and precisely. Not wavering one way or the other. While most students struggle to find the path to who they are, I have a feeling Bruce already knows what he wants. And that can be a dangerous thing.

Special Notes:
I hesitate to answer if Bruce is a worthy candidate for Nanda Parbat. I will continue to keep a close eye on him before making a final determination.

I was able to infiltrate and make a copy of this for my own files without being noticed. The following is security cam footage from before I deleted it from the school system.

What is "Nanda Parbat"? This name requires further investigating. —B

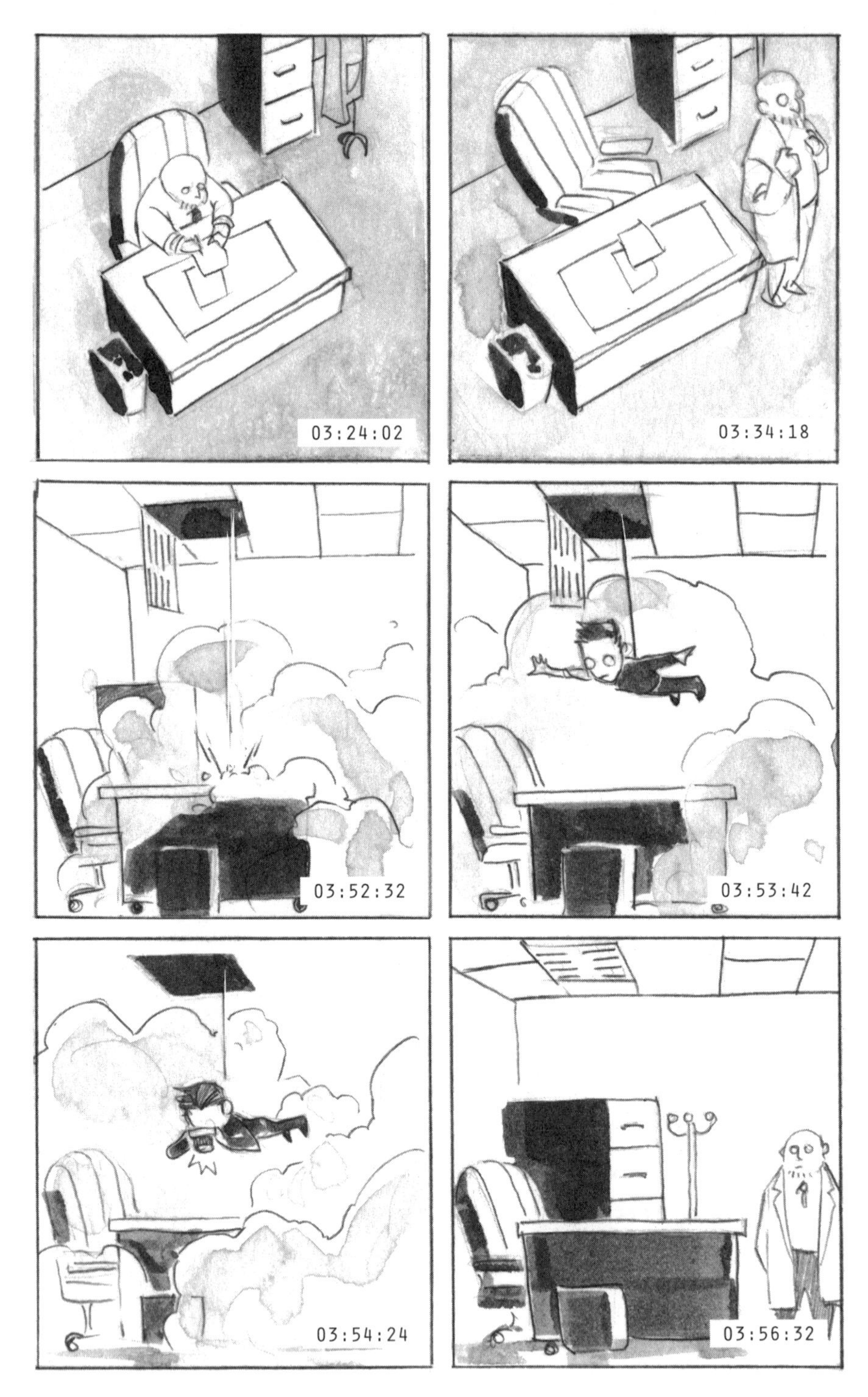
03:24:02
03:34:18
03:52:32
03:53:42
03:54:24
03:56:32

THE DUCARD DAILY

OCTOBER 13

SCHOOL NEWSPAPER STAFF

VICTOR FRIES/WEATHER

"Freeze" reports the latest cold snap

CIRCE/HOROSCOPE

Bringing your weekly dose of horror

PAMELA ISLEY/
STAFF ENVIRONMENTAL REPORTER

Nature is nurture

HELLO, EVERYONE. MY NAME IS CLARK KENT. AND I'D LIKE TO BECOME A REPORTER FOR THE SCHOOL NEWSPAPER!
YOU'RE PAMELA ISLEY—
CALL ME POISON IVY.
UM . . . I KINDA LIKE PAM BETTER. AND YOU WRITE ARTICLES ABOUT THE ENVIRONMENT. THAT'S GOOD.
WE HAVEN'T MET. I'M CLARK.
"FREEZE." VICTOR FRIES. I HANDLE THE WEATHER COLUMN.
THAT'S COOL!
A PUN. I'D LAUGH IF I CARED.
I'M CIRCE. I HANDLE THE HOROSCOPES. WHAT'S YOUR SIGN?
I'M NOT SURE, I—

WHY ARE TOMORROW'S TEST ANSWERS PRINTED HERE?
IS THAT THE ONLY "NEWS" YOU PRINT— DISHONESTY AND DISASTER?
WHAT HAPPENED TO REPORTING EVENTS? HUMAN INTEREST? A SIT-DOWN WITH THE PRINCIPAL? PROFILES ON EXCEPTIONAL STUDENTS?
DON'T WORRY. I'LL GET OUT THERE AND REPORT THE NEWS. YOU CAN COUNT ON ME!
HE REALLY SHOULD HAVE TAKEN A JACKET. THE FORECAST IS SUPPOSED TO BE . . . COLD.

THE DUCARD DAILY

OCTOBER 15

WEATHER REPORT

Victor Fries/Meteorologist

Cloudy 42°

Wind: 20 MPH

Chance of snow: Extremely likely

Fries's 5-Day Forecast: Rain, sleet, snow, snow, snow

PLANTS ARE BETTER THAN PEOPLE

Pamela Isley/
Staff Environmental Reporter
see page 4

HORROR SCOPES

by **Circe**

Cloudy days are ahead . . . rejoice! Every goal is within your grasp for the taking. Set your ideas into motion. Don't wait for the storm to pass . . . BE the storm! Seize the day by force. And if anyone tries to stop you, just tell them you get to do whatever you want.

UP, UP, AND AWAY!

by **Clark Kent** / Staff Reporter

As the newest journalist, I'd like to take this time to introduce myself. Growing up in Smallville, I learned many valuable lessons that would (continued on pg Z17)

AT THE PRINCIPAL'S OFFICE . . .
HI. IS THE PRINCIPAL AVAILABLE?
WHO ARE YOU?
CLARK KENT. THE NEW STAFF REPORTER.
YOU MIGHT'VE HEARD OF ME. MY LATEST ARTICLE MADE THE BACK PAGE. *WAAAY* IN THE BACK.
NO.
THE PRINCIPAL ONLY MEETS WITH THOSE HE DEEMS WORTHY. NO PRESS!
YOU CAN ONLY BE IN THE OFFICE IF YOU HAVE A SCHEDULED APPOINTMENT OR IF YOU'RE THE CLASS PRESIDENT. OTHERWISE . . . SCRAM!
HMM . . . *CLASS PRESIDENT!*

GIRLS' SPORTS SYLLABUS

Physical Fitness and Obedience Rules

by

COACH "KITTY" FAULKNER

THE DOS AND DON'TS TO PULVERIZE YOUR OPPONENT:

- DO fight
- DO cheat
- DO steal

- DON'T play fair
- DON'T be a good sport

GIVE OUT DISCIPLINE OR BE DISCIPLINED!!!

TRYING OUT FOR THE TEAM?
CORRECT. THAT IS WHY WE'RE ALL HERE, RIGHT?
WATCH YOUR BACK.
HISS!
READY . . . GET SET . . .
OKAY, LADIES AND GERMS, LINE UP!

HEY! HANDS OFF THE EARS, KITTY CAT!
I SAW WHAT SHE DID. HERE, LET ME—
TRIP!
NICE ONE, GIGANTA!
GREAT HERA! HOW?! WHAT MAGIC MADE HER GROW LIKE THAT?
FACE IT. YOU LOST, PRINCESS! AND YOU'RE CUT FROM THE TEAM.

STUDENT EVALUATION REPORT

STUDENT: Diana Prince **PROFESSOR:** Hugo Strange

Which of the following best describes you?
Choose only one:

❑ Ambitious ☒ Angry ❑ Bored ❑ Calm ❑ Confused ❑ Creative ❑ Embarrassed
❑ Excited ❑ Focused ❑ Happy ❑ Hungry ❑ Lonely ❑ Loved ❑ Patient
❑ Proud ❑ Relieved ❑ Sad ❑ Scared ❑ Surprised ❑ Tired ❑ Other

Please rate the following based on how you are feeling about each area of your life:

Friendships
Terrible 1 2 (3) 4 5 6 7 8 9 10 Great

Home/Family
Terrible 1 2 3 4 5 6 (7) 8 9 10 Great

Grades/School
Terrible 1 2 3 (4) 5 6 7 8 9 10 Great

Diagnosis:
As a foreign exchange student, Diana struggles to fit in and belong. This may be due to a sheltered upbringing or royal heritage. She holds herself to a higher standard and falls short. Her weakness is her unwavering nobility and fairness. But her strength is her quick-tempered anger, which we can greatly exploit.

Special Notes:
She is a strong possibility for Nanda Parbat, but must be pushed further for us to be absolutely certain.

That name again, "Nanda Parbat." This can't be a coincidence. High priority to find out what it means!

—B

DATE: OCTOBER 20

USERNAME: BWAYNE

RE: JOURNAL ENTRY 8

OUR SECOND MISSIONS WEREN'T ANY BETTER.

CLARK JOINED THE SCHOOL NEWSPAPER. BUT ANYTHING HE WRITES GETS MOVED TO THE LAST PAGE. MOST ISN'T EVEN PRINTED. THEY SEEM TO ONLY WRITE ABOUT MEAN THINGS AND WEIRDNESS. AND HE'S TOO NICE TO REALIZE HE'S WASTING HIS TIME.

BUT HE CAME UP WITH THE IDEA OF RUNNING FOR CLASS PRESIDENT. NOT A BAD IDEA! IT'LL ALLOW HIM ACCESS TO THE SCHOOL OFFICE IF HE WINS.

DIANA WAS CUT FROM THE ATHLETICS TEAM. SHE WAS SO MAD THAT I COULD HEAR HER YELLING ACROSS CAMPUS. I ADMIRE HER DETERMINATION, BUT NOT HER TEMPER.

I'VE DECIDED TO MAKE HER CLARK'S CAMPAIGN MANAGER. THAT WAY, SHE CAN FOCUS ON GETTING THE FARM BOY ELECTED.

I'M STILL INVESTIGATING THE PHRASE "NANDA PARBAT." SO FAR I'M HITTING DEAD ENDS, BUT IT'S THE ONLY LEAD I HAVE.

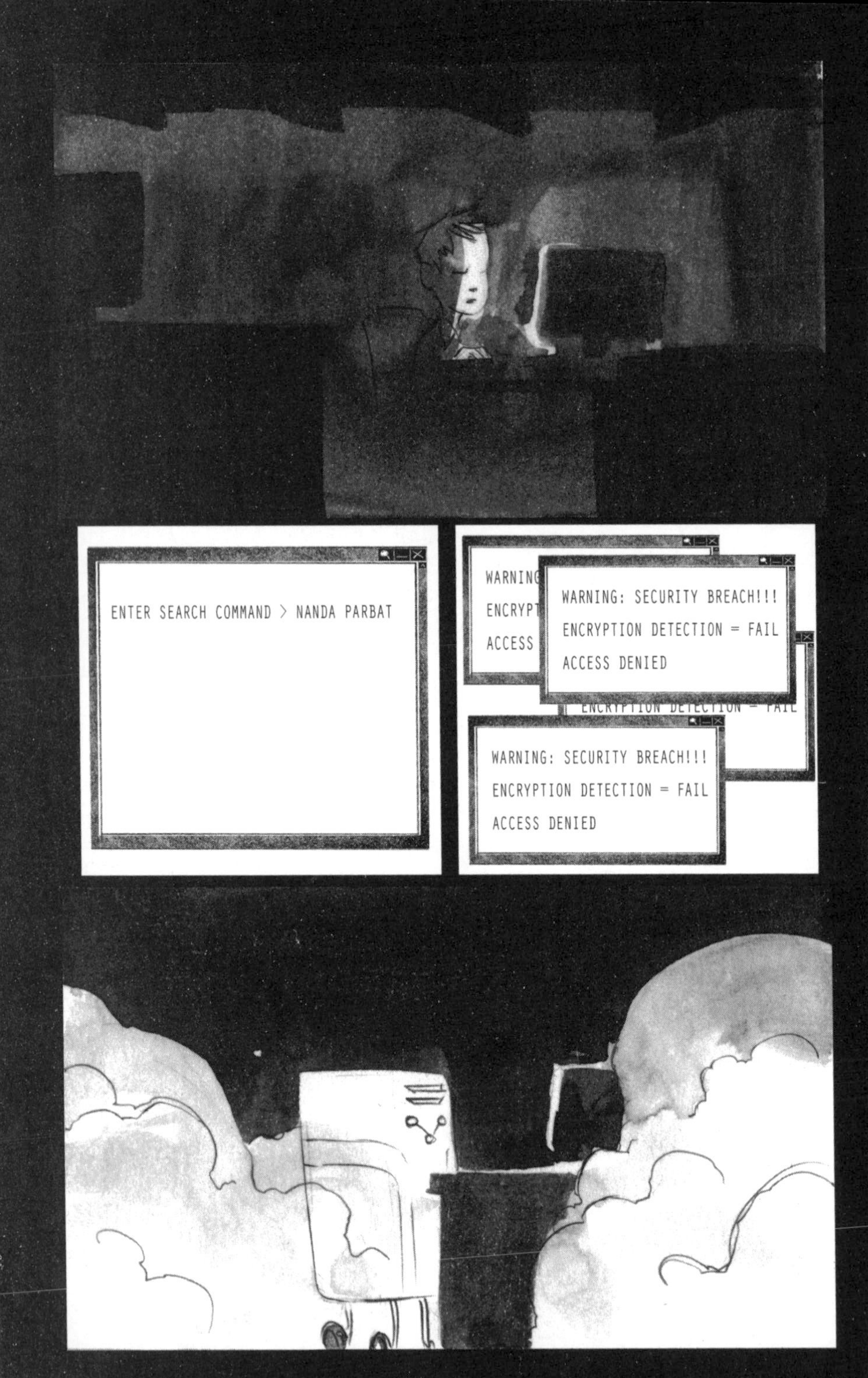
ENTER SEARCH COMMAND > NANDA PARBAT
WARNING: SECURITY BREACH!!!
ENCRYPTION DETECTION = FAIL
ACCESS DENIED
WARNING: SECURITY BREACH!!!
ENCRYPTION DETECTION = FAIL
ACCESS DENIED

Okay, ghouls and goblins. Tomorrow's Halloween!

Time to ditch your school clothes and dress accordingly. Taunt, scare, and get into trouble . . . It's what you're supposed to do.

Don't smash any pumpkins, or face my wrath!!!

— **Pamela Isley**/Staff Environmental Reporter

MESSAGES
GROUP CHAT
clark, diana, we need to talk.
what time tomorrow?
no, now, things are more dangerous, we might be compromised.
What did u do this time? :/
i may have tripped some alarms.
how?
trying to access information on the school computers, a stupid mistake.
but u don't make those.
. . . i think i'm being followed, we all might be.
SEND

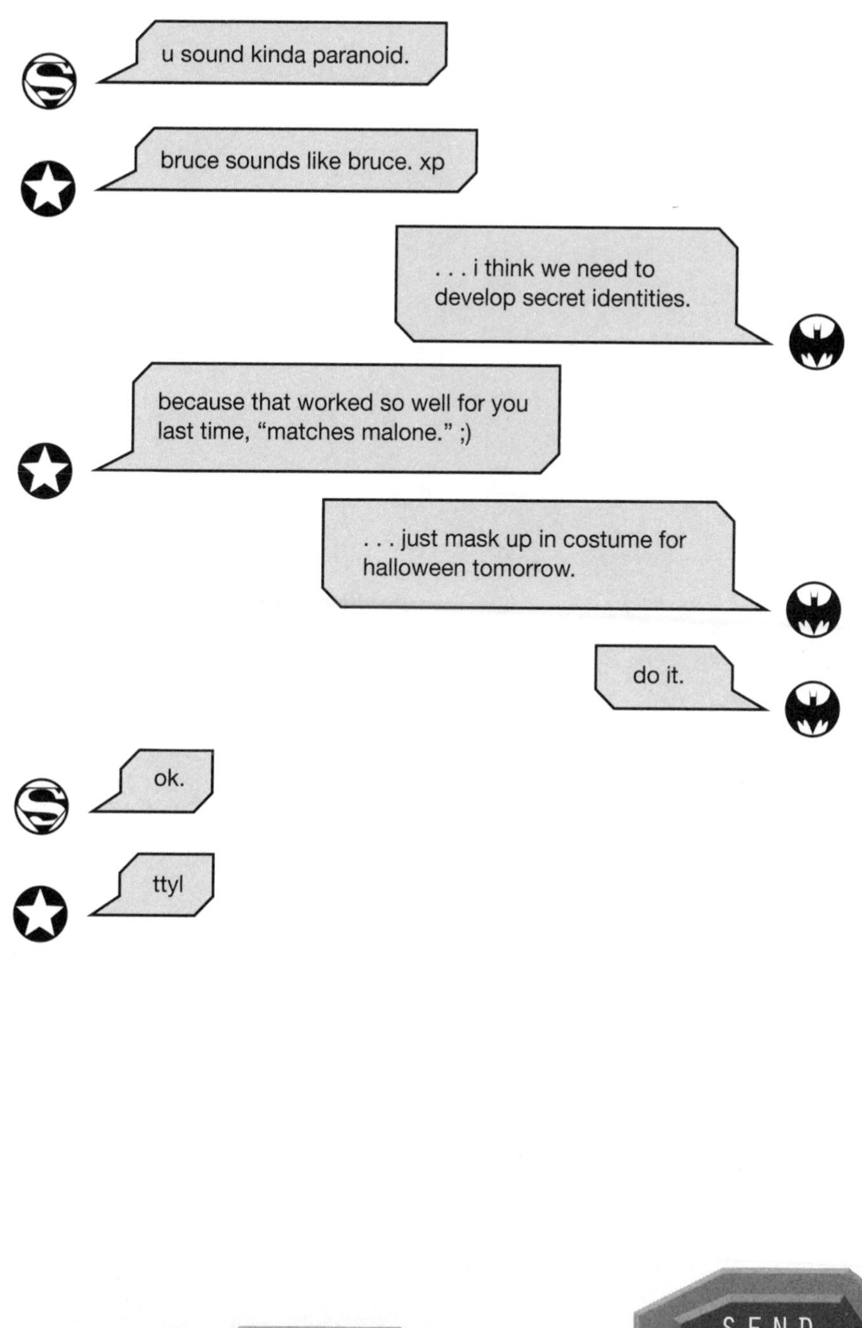
MESSAGES
GROUP CHAT
u sound kinda paranoid.
bruce sounds like bruce. xp
. . . i think we need to develop secret identities.
because that worked so well for you last time, “matches malone.” ;)
. . . just mask up in costume for halloween tomorrow.
do it.
ok.
ttyl
SEND

OCTOBER 31—HALLOWEEN

ARE YOU SURE HE MEANT TODAY?
HE'LL BE HERE.
HA-HA-HA-HA!
WHAT ARE YOU SUPPOSED TO BE?
BATMAN.
BAT . . . *WHO?*
IT'S SUPPOSED TO STRIKE FEAR. I . . . LIKE BATS.

FINE! THEN WHAT ARE YOU BOTH SUPPOSED TO BE?
WHAT DOES THE "S" STAND FOR?
OH, IT'S FROM MY HOME PLANET . . . ER, I MEAN HOMETOWN . . . YEAH, "S" IS FOR SMALLVILLE.
I LIKE IT!
HE STILL LOOKS THE SAME, EVEN WITHOUT GLASSES. WHERE'S THE MASK?
I AM AN AMAZON WARRIOR!
YOU LOOK WONDERFUL.
YOU'RE NOT WEARING A MASK, EITHER?
GRUMBLE . . .

TIRED OF WORKING ALONE TO
RULE THE WORLD?

SEEKING INJUSTICE IN
A JUST SOCIETY?

LET'S GANG TOGETHER AND
COME UP WITH THE SOLUTION!

I FOUND THIS CIRCULATING ON CAMPUS.
I DON'T LIKE THE SOUND OF THIS.
IT'S A GREAT DAY TO BE EVIL!
OR THE SOUND OF THAT.
WHAT'S OUR PURPOSE HERE?
TO CAUSE CHAOS, OF COURSE!
GOOD. I STARTED BY STEALING ALL THE CANDY. HEE-HEE!
YOU'RE THINKING TOO SMALL. WHY CAN'T WE EXPAND OUR OPERATION OUTSIDE OF SCHOOL? STEAL SCIENTIFIC EQUIPMENT.
OR ANCIENT ARTIFACTS!
BANK ROBBERIES!
EVERYTHING DUCARD IS PREPARING US FOR.

BAM!
WE HEARD EVERYTHING. NOT BECAUSE OF SUPER-HEARING OR ANYTHING. BUT JUST BECAUSE WE WERE NEARBY AND—
SHUT UP AND FIGHT!
WHAT HE SAID!
LIBRARY IS CLOSED.
LEAVE NOW.
BONK!
KEEP AN EYE ON THOSE THREE ESPECIALLY.
CONFIRMED.

DATE: NOVEMBER 1

USERNAME: BWAYNE

RE: JOURNAL ENTRY 9

HALLOWEEN REVEALED A LOT TO ME.

THE STUDENTS REALLY LIKED DRESSING UP. NOT BECAUSE OF THE HOLIDAY. BUT TO GET INTO TROUBLE. THEY SHOWED THEIR TRUE COLORS.

MY FRIENDS' COSTUMES NEED WORK. THEY NEED MASKS! OTHERWISE, EVERYONE WILL RECOGNIZE THEM. BUT AT LEAST THEY'RE PLAYING ALONG.

WHO IS CLARK KENT, REALLY? HE'S MORE THAN A FARM KID. BUT HE'S TOO GOOD TO LIE. WHAT'S HE HIDING?

AND DIANA HAS SOMETHING ELSE GOING ON, TOO. SHE'S STRONGER THAN EVERYONE ELSE. AND THAT CROWN SHE WEARS LOOKS ROYAL. WHAT ISLAND IS SHE FROM?

HOW WILL I FIND TIME TO INVESTIGATE THE SCHOOL AND MY FRIENDS?

CLARK KENT
FOR
CLASS PRESIDENT
PREZ

HALLWAY-MONITOR 04
15:21:14

HALLWAY-MONITOR 03
15:22:02

HALLWAY-MONITOR 04
15:22:46

HALLWAY-MONITOR 04
15:23:12

HALLWAY-MONITOR 02
15:23:41

HALLWAY-MONITOR 03
15:24:16

HALLWAY-MONITOR 02
15:24:32

HALLWAY-MONITOR 01
15:25:03

VOTE
LEX
FOR CLASS
PRESIDENT

NOVEMBER 4

CLARK KENT VS. LEX LUTHOR

PRESIDENTIAL DEBATE TOMORROW!

WEATHER REPORT

Victor Fries/Meteorologist

Overcast 30°

Wind: 10 MPH

Fries's 5-Day Forecast: Frosty

HORROR SCOPES

by **Circe**

The future looks bright . . . Don't let it be. Don't listen to others. Your vote is all that matters. Be your own leader. And remember, it's what's on the outside that counts!

Cast your vote with your voice instead of a ballot. Save a tree!!!!!

— **Pamela Isley**/Staff Environmental Reporter

CLARK, AS YOUR CAMPAIGN MANAGER, I THINK WE NEED TO HEAR WHAT YOU'RE GOING TO SAY IN THE DEBATE TOMORROW.
I STAND FOR TRUTH AND JUSTICE!
HEY, "BOY SCOUT"! YOUR NEWSPAPER ARTICLES STINK!

FIZZZ!
. . .
CLARK, HOW DID YOU DO THAT?!
I . . . I DON'T KNOW.
TRY NOT TO DO *THAT* IN THE DEBATE.

DATE: NOVEMBER 4

USERNAME: BWAYNE

RE: JOURNAL ENTRY 10

CLARK CONTINUES TO STRUGGLE PRESENTING HIMSELF AS THE BEST OPTION FOR CLASS PRESIDENT. IT DIDN'T TAKE MUCH TO UPSET HIM. WHAT I DIDN'T EXPECT WAS HOW HE'D REACT.

LASER-BEAM EYES? FURTHER FUELING MY SUSPICIONS THAT CLARK IS NOT WHO OR WHAT HE APPEARS TO BE.

AT LEAST HE'S ON OUR SIDE. IF NOT, I'LL HAVE TO FIND OUT HIS WEAKNESS. MINE IS CHOCOLATE CHIP COOKIES. (ALFRED—IF YOU'RE READING THIS . . . TAKE ADVANTAGE OF MY WEAKNESS!)

SPEECH LIST

Tell the truth.

Don't be afraid to avoid questions.

Present what you stand for.

Say what they want to hear.

Emphasize your best qualities.

Don't be snobby.

Just be yourself.

Be who they want you to be.

They want you to be more like THEM. Play along.

Photos–Ducard Presidential Debate

Our candidates take the stage.

"I'm a farm boy from Smallville, I wanna do good things."

"Good things? Boring . . ."

Lex knows what the crowd wants.

"Lex! Lex! Lex!"

Lex made Clarky cry.

Campaign advisor Diana clearly telling him to vote Lex!

His own team agrees. VOTE LEX!

The farm boy claims Lex is a cheater and has proof. Yeaaaaah, riiiiight.

REPORT CARD

STUDENT: Lex Luthor **HOMEROOM:**
LEVEL: **SEMESTER:**

Subject	Grade	Teacher Notes
ENGLISH	A+++	Now you're speaking my language $$$ Thx!
MATH	A+++	Computer hacking shows initiative. Well done!
SCIENCE	A++++	I gave you one extra plus. Or maybe you did? Quite the mad scientist!
ART	A+++	Thanks for your generous donation to me. You passed with flying colors.
HISTORY	A+++	You've learned the greatest historical lesson: *Money is power.*

STUDYING AND HARD WORK SHOULD BE REWARDED.
WE SHOULDN'T REWARD BRIBERY OR TRICKS.

I ASK YOU THIS, STUDENTS OF DUCARD: DO YOU WANT TO VOTE FOR SOMEONE TRULY HONEST . . .
. . . OR THE OTHER GUY WHO WILL LIE, CHEAT, AND STEAL TO GET WHAT HE WANTS?
THE CHOICE IS UP TO YOU.
FREE PIZZA AND ICE CREAM FOR EVERYONE! MY TREAT!

THE DUCARD DAILY

NOVEMBER 6

ELECTION RESULTS:

NEW CLASS PRESIDENT WINS IN LANDSLIDE!!!

"Grumble, grumble . . . Hey, don't print that!" says loser Clark Kent.

STUDENT EVALUATION REPORT

STUDENT: Clark Kent **PROFESSOR:** Hugo Strange

Which of the following best describes you?
Choose only one:

☒ Ambitious ❑ Angry ❑ Bored ❑ Calm ❑ Confused ❑ Creative ❑ Embarrassed
❑ Excited ❑ Focused ❑ Happy ❑ Hungry ❑ Lonely ❑ Loved ❑ Patient
❑ Proud ❑ Relieved ❑ Sad ❑ Scared ❑ Surprised ❑ Tired ❑ Other

Please rate the following based on how you are feeling about each area of your life:

Friendships
Terrible ... Great
1 2 (3) 4 5 6 7 8 9 10

Home/Family
Terrible ... Great
1 2 3 4 5 6 7 8 9 (10)

Grades/School
Terrible ... Great
1 2 3 4 5 6 (7) 8 9 10

Diagnosis:
Clark is eager to please others. To be the best and rise above everyone, to be a great role model. But is that what we're looking for? No one is perfect. Everyone has some weakness. But so far, no one has been able to find any. Losing the election should've knocked him down a notch. But he seems as upbeat as ever. It's troubling.

Special Notes:
His power can help our cause or hurt us. If we can't work with him, then we must work against him.

This confirms my suspicions that Clark is of alien origin. If they're afraid of him, that has to be a good thing, as long as he stays on the side of good.
—B

LATER, AT LUNCH . . .
HEY, LOOK . . . APPLESAUCE! ENOUGH HERE FOR EVERYONE.
YOU PLAYED RIGHT INTO LEX'S HANDS, WHICH IS WHY YOU LOST. YOU DIDN'T EVEN TRY TO BEND YOUR SPEECH OR PLATFORM TO FIT THE REST OF THE SCHOOL.
I CAN'T BE ANYONE BUT MYSELF.
I FIND THAT HARD TO BELIEVE, *ALIEN*.
WHAT?!
SMASH!

UGH . . . BOYS!! YOU BOTH ARE TOO STUBBORN TO LISTEN TO ANYONE BUT YOURSELVES.
I SHOULD'VE NEVER LEFT THEMYSCIRA. IT'S A PARADISE COMPARED TO HERE.
THEN WHY DON'T YOU GO BACK TO YOUR HIDDEN ISLAND?!
YEAH . . . I INVESTIGATED YOU, TOO!
UNLESS ANYONE HAS ANY OBJECTIONS, I'M DISSOLVING THE CIU, EFFECTIVE IMMEDIATELY.
FINE!
AGREED!
REFRAIN FROM DESTROYING SCHOOL PROPERTY.

DATE: NOVEMBER 15

USERNAME: BWAYNE

RE: JOURNAL ENTRY 11

I KNOW NOW THAT EVERYONE WAS BROUGHT TOGETHER FOR A REASON. THAT MUCH IS FOR CERTAIN. BUT FIGURING THIS OUT HAS CAUSED TROUBLE.

TODAY I CLOSED OUR CRIMINAL INVESTIGATION UNIT. IT WASN'T WORKING. EACH OF US HAS OUR OWN SECRETS. AND WORKING TOGETHER IS NO LONGER A PRIORITY.

I WAS HOPING FOR PARTNERS, FELLOW INVESTIGATORS, EVEN FRIENDS. BUT I FEAR I HAVE NONE OF THOSE ANYMORE.

MAYBE IT'S FOR THE BEST. I'M BUMMED NOT TO HAVE SOMEONE TO HANG OUT WITH AND TALK STRATEGY . . . OR EVEN VIDEO GAMES. BUT I'LL JUST DO IT ALONE. I'M USED TO THAT.

I JUST NEED A NEW PLACE TO DO MY WORK. THE LIBRARY NO LONGER FEELS RIGHT.

NEW POSSIBLE LOCATIONS FOR SECRET HEADQUARTERS:

- RESTROOM (unfavorable odor and an accident waiting to happen)
- BASEBALL BACKSTOP (Selina and her gang of friends hang out there often)
- CAFETERIA DUMPSTER (pros: food access; cons: garbage)
- BEHIND THE MUSIC BUILDING (noise not conducive to my work)
- COMPUTER ROOM (access to information, but raises awareness)
- SCIENCE LAB (great for forensics, but Lex around too much)

Keep looking . . .

DATE: NOVEMBER 20

USERNAME: BWAYNE

RE: JOURNAL ENTRY 12

WITH THE LIBRARY ABANDONED AFTER DISBANDING THE CRIMINAL INVESTIGATION UNIT, I HAVE DECIDED UPON A NEW LOCATION TO CONTINUE MY WORK ALONE. I'VE SELECTED THE JANITOR'S BASEMENT. LOCATED UNDER THE SCHOOL AWAY FROM SPYING EYES, IT'S THE PERFECT SPOT. CURRENTLY, IT IS USED AS A STORAGE FACILITY FOR SCHOOL AND OFFICE SUPPLIES, GARDENING EQUIPMENT, AND BATHROOM ITEMS. BUT NO ONE EVER COMES DOWN HERE. IT'S AS SAFE A PLACE AS ANY TO WORK FOR NOW.

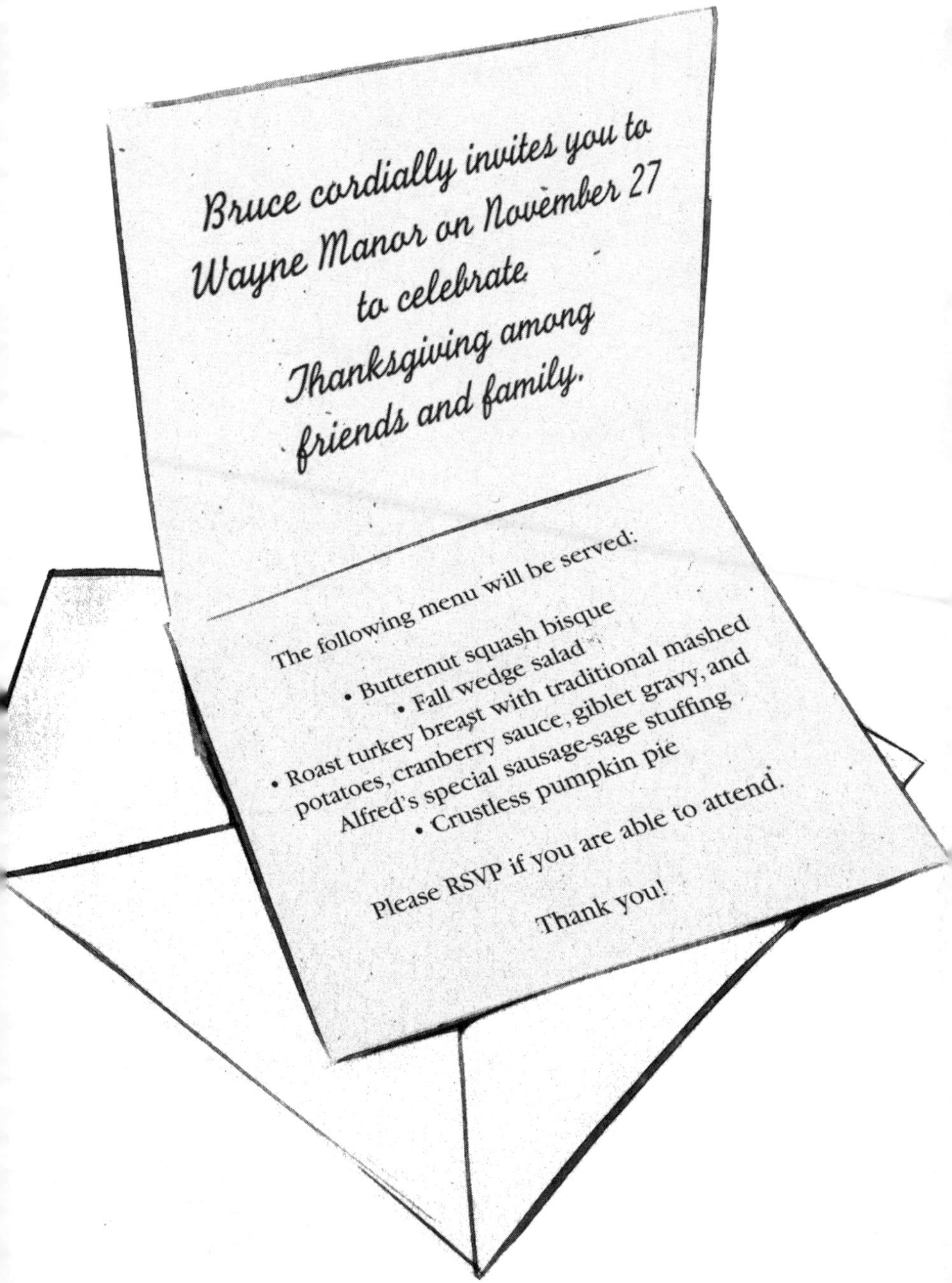

Bruce cordially invites you to Wayne Manor on November 27 to celebrate Thanksgiving among friends and family.

The following menu will be served:

• Butternut squash bisque
• Fall wedge salad
• Roast turkey breast with traditional mashed potatoes, cranberry sauce, giblet gravy, and Alfred's special sausage-sage stuffing
• Crustless pumpkin pie

Please RSVP if you are able to attend.

Thank you!

THANKSGIVING . . .
RSVP
RSVP

IT'S A SHAME NONE OF YOUR FRIENDS COULD JOIN US.
THEY WERE ALL BUSY OR SOMETHING. IT DOESN'T MATTER.
FRIENDSHIPS ARE ABOUT ACCEPTING OUR DIFFERENCES AS WELL AS OUR SIMILARITIES.
WHEN WE DO THAT, WE'RE ABLE TO BECOME SOMETHING GREATER AS A WHOLE THAN WE ARE APART. A TRUE FRIEND.
HAPPY THANKSGIVING, ALFRED.
AND TO YOU AS WELL, MASTER BRUCE.

LATER, IN GYM CLASS . . .
WELCOME TO BOYS' PHYSICAL EDUCATION.
KNEEL BEFORE COACH ZOD!
TOO GOOD TO BEND A KNEE, WAYNE?
VERY WELL, THEN, YOU'LL BEND TO MY PRIZED WRESTLING STUDENT . . . BANE!
BRUCE WAYNE? MORE LIKE BRUCE *PAIN*, AMIGO!

LEAVE HIM ALONE!
CATCH THIS!
DON'T STAND OUT! ACT NORMAL!
OH, YEAH . . .
OOF.

SCHOOL NURSE INCIDENT REPORT

STUDENT: Bryce Wayne

TEACHER: Coach Zod

CLASS: Boys' PE

DATE: December 1

DESCRIPTION OF THE INCIDENT:

There was a fight in class. Some students started wrestling with one another. Bruce appears to have a sore head. Clark Kent and Bane were also involved.

ACTION TAKEN:

Each student was examined and treated. Following that, Bruce was sent to detention. Clark spoke of a stomachache, but was not very convincing, and was also given detention.

FURTHER RECOMMENDED CARE:

None.

NOTES:

He possesses remarkable strength for his age. Perhaps he is extraordinary in other ways, too.

IF YOU HAVE ANY QUESTIONS ABOUT THIS EVENT, PLEASE CALL THE NURSE'S OFFICE.

Diana Prince
December 1

GIRLS' PHYSICAL EDUCATION—POP QUIZ

COACH "**KITTY**" FAULKNER Class of Hard Knocks

If someone steals money out of your locker during class, and you find out who did it, what do you do?

It is wrong to steal. And violence should be avoided. There can always be more peaceful options. Confront and talk to them. Work it out. You might end up becoming friends.

ALL RIGHT, GIRLS. YOU'RE THE LAST ONES LEFT. LAST GIRL STANDING, WINS.
I'VE BEEN WAITING A LONG TIME FOR THIS, OUTSIDER!
I HAVE NO QUARREL WITH YOU. PERHAPS IF WE TALK—
WORDS WILL NOT HURT ME!

BUT THEY WILL HURT YOU . . .
LOOK! HER FACE IS GETTING ALL RED. NOW, THAT'S FUNNY!
DON'T TRIP UP WITH YOUR GIRAFFE LEGS!
DIANA BANANA!!
TALIA WINS!
ARGHHH!

I HEAR THAT YOU'VE EXCELLED IN YOUR ATHLETICS AND STUDIES. TODAY YOU EVEN BESTED THE AMAZON. A RARE AND WORTHY ACCOMPLISHMENT!
YOU'VE EARNED THIS MEDAL. AND MY ADMIRATION.
THANK YOU, F—
SHH, PLEASE!
NO NEED TO ADDRESS ME BY NAME. NOT WITH SO MANY EYES AND EARS OUT THERE.
CONSIDER THIS THE FIRST OF MANY WAYS TO MAKE ME PROUD. THERE WILL BE OTHERS.

OFFICE—INCIDENT REPORT

STUDENT: DIANA PRINCE

DATE: DECEMBER 2

LOCATION: GIRLS' PE

INCIDENT:

Student is filing a complaint of cheating and name-calling committed by the other students in class. Also for the coach allowing it to happen. When confronted, the coach said that when competing against others, there's no such thing as unfair. The student disagreed and was given detention.

Found this filed away in the office while investigating. It's good to read that Diana continues even if we are no longer a team.

—B

WELCOME TO DETENTION.
FOR THE NEXT WEEK
I WILL CONTROL ALL THAT YOU SEE OR HEAR.
I CAN'T BELIEVE I'M IN HERE WITH YOU TWO.
IT WASN'T ON PURPOSE, I CAN TELL YOU THAT MUCH.
THIS IS JUST LIKE THEM TO—
SILENCE.
I HAVE MANY TASKS THAT REQUIRE COMPLETION.
DO AS I COMMAND.

DATE: DECEMBER 3

USERNAME: BWAYNE

RE: JOURNAL ENTRY 13

SO . . . I'M STUCK IN AFTER-SCHOOL DETENTION FOR A WEEK. ALFRED IS DISAPPOINTED IN ME. I THINK BECAUSE MY CHORES ARE NOW DELAYED. RIGHT?

DETENTION IS A WASTE OF TIME. BRAINIAC HAS GIVEN US TASKS TO KEEP US BUSY. FILING PAPERWORK, CATEGORIZING THE LIBRARY, RETURNING BOOKS, AND SEEKING BACKGROUND INFORMATION ON OTHER STUDENTS.

I NEED TO FIND A WAY OUT!!!

I DID MANAGE TO SNEAK IN A SMALL HIDDEN CAMERA AND WAS ABLE TO TAKE PICTURES. I STILL SPOT NINJA, BOTH AROUND CAMPUS AND NOW IN THE LIBRARY. THEY ARE EVERYWHERE! MAYBE I NEED TO TRACK THEM INSTEAD.

VIEW ACTIVITY LOG_FOE REQUESTS_MAIL
<GLOOMBOOK LOGIN PROTOCOL ACHIEVED>
<POKE REQUEST>

 Hey, you guys there?

 Here

 What do YOU want?

 I know you don't want to talk, but we really need to.

 BRAINIAC has been making me file paperwork. But really he's probing me for information about the two of you.

 He asked about you as well.

Yeah. So?

We have to get out of here. But to do so, we'll have to work together.

GLOOMBOOK

Because that worked so well the last time >:(

It beats bookkeeping. So what's the plan?

We need to distract him.

What good is that if we can't get out? Remember those doors are electronically locked and controlled by BRAINIAC.

Can we shut off BRAINIAC? He must have an off switch.

Not without drawing attention.

So we've got nothing.

For now. But tomorrow we can—

YOU ARE UNAUTHORIZED TO BE HERE
ACCESS DENIED

<SESSION CLOSED>

DATE: DECEMBER 4

USERNAME: BWAYNE

RE: JOURNAL ENTRY 14

IT'S NOT FUN, BUT I'M TEAMED UP WITH CLARK AND DIANA AGAIN. IT'S THE ONLY WAY WE CAN WORK TOWARD ESCAPING DETENTION.

SO FAR, WE'VE BEEN UNSUCCESSFUL. EVERY WAY OUT APPEARS TO BE BLOCKED BY BRAINIAC. HE ELECTRONICALLY LOCKS THE DOORS. THE ELECTRICAL MAINFRAME OF THE BUILDING RUNS THROUGH HIS SYSTEM. WE CAN'T ACCESS THE COMPUTERS IN THE LIBRARY. AND HE'S CONSTANTLY WATCHING EVERYTHING WE DO AND KEEPING US WORKING.

I BELIEVE I HAVE A PLAN TO GET US OUT. BUT IT REQUIRES A LITTLE MAPMAKING, SOME TIMING, AND A LOT OF LUCK. I'LL PRESENT IT TO THE OTHERS TOMORROW AND SEE WHAT THEY THINK.

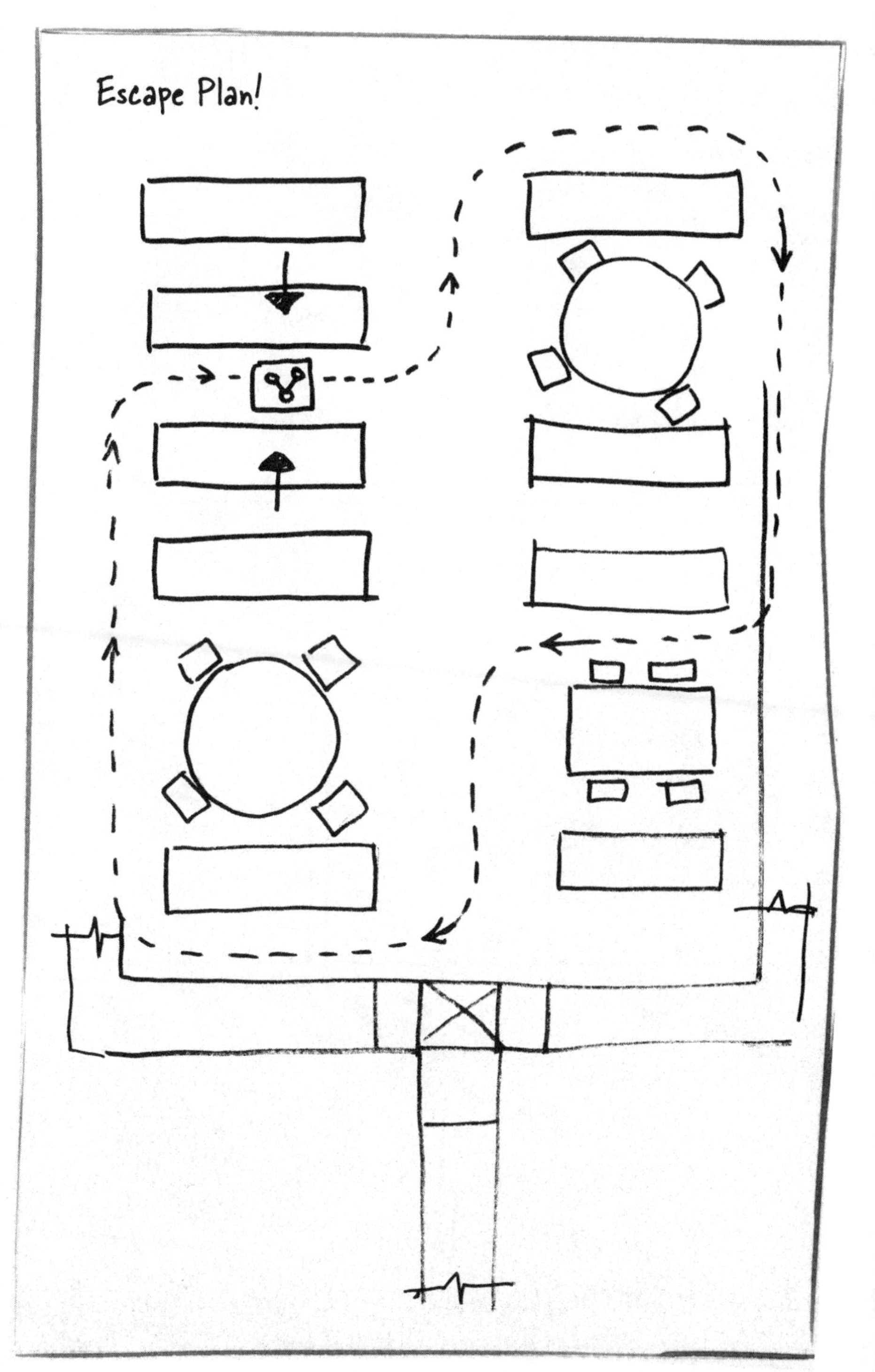
Escape Plan!

ACCESS SEARCH PROGRAM.
LOADING . . .
THUNK!

THIS IS EXCITING!
SHHH!
WHERE ARE WE?
THE JANITOR'S BASEMENT UNDER THE SCHOOL. I'VE BEEN USING IT AS MY TEMPORARY HIDEOUT TO WORK AFTER THE LIBRARY BECAME UNUSABLE.
WHAT DO YOU THINK?
IT'S DARK AND DANK LIKE A CAVE DOWN HERE.
I KNOW! ISN'T IT PERFECT?!

DATE: DECEMBER 5

USERNAME: BWAYNE

RE: JOURNAL ENTRY 15

KNOWING HOW BAD BEHAVIOR IS REWARDED AT DUCARD, WE'VE BEEN PRAISED AND LEFT ALONE AFTER OUR SUCCESSFUL BREAKOUT FROM DETENTION.

I'VE DECIDED TO RE-FORM THE CRIMINAL INVESTIGATION UNIT. HAVING PATCHED THINGS UP, I'M HAPPY TO BE WITH MY FRIENDS AGAIN. EVEN THOUGH I'M FULLY EQUIPPED TO WORK ALONE. I'M JUST SAYING.

OUR NEW MISSION IS TO GO DIRECTLY TO THE TOP. WHO IS THE MASTERMIND BEHIND THIS SCHOOL AND WHAT IS THEIR ENDGAME? SOMEONE IS PULLING EVERYONE'S STRINGS BUT DOES SO FROM THE SHADOWS. IT'S TIME TO LURE THEM OUT AND SEE WHO THEY ARE.

DUCARD HOLIDAY PROGRAM

DECEMBER 15

8:00 P.M.—DUCARD AUDITORIUM

'Tis the season . . .
Come join us for a little bit of holiday doom and gloom.
Our students are prepared to put on a program with singing, dancing, and festive decorations.

Cookie and candy snacks will be provided to all your li'l bad boys and girls after the concert.

Join us and help celebrate!

SPLAT!
SMAK!

ANSWER ME!
WHO'S THROWING SNOWBALLS?!
SKREEEEEE!
SHE'S QUITE THE SILVER BANSHEE! HEE-HEE-HEEEE!
TREES AND LEAVES ARE NOT DECORATIONS FOR YOUR AMUSEMENT!

THE DUCARD DAILY

DECEMBER 18

LETTER FROM THE PRESIDENT

by Lex Luthor

As winter break approaches, I wish all of you time off to rest and enjoy the coming of the new year. And for all your mad desires to be fulfilled. There's lots to conquer next year.
Let's get to it!

THERE'S NO DAY LIKE A SNOW DAY.
SEE YOU NEXT WINTER . . .

—Victor Fries

apons trainin
h Artemis
wn with Alfred.
Merry Christmas from Paradise!

new puppy!
made a
boome
ther cool cave
he east wing!
working on my ~~spaceship~~
tractor.

DATE: JANUARY 5

USERNAME: BWAYNE

RE: JOURNAL ENTRY 16

WINTER BREAK IS COMING TO AN END AND SCHOOL STARTS TOMORROW. WHILE OTHERS SPENT THEIR TIME WITH THEIR FAMILIES AND TRAVELING, I DECIDED TO STAY IN THE MANSION AND CONTINUE MY INVESTIGATIONS INTO THE SCHOOL. I ALSO FOUND TIME TO TRY OUT MY NEW SLED AND ALFRED'S SNOWMOBILE (BUT DON'T TELL HIM).

I'VE BEEN ABLE TO NARROW "NANDA PARBAT" AS A LOCATION. BUT NOT SPECIFICALLY WHERE. I'VE EXHAUSTED ALL MEANS ON MY COMPUTER. I MAY HAVE TO SEEK ALTERNATIVE MEANS I'VE NEVER CONSIDERED BEFORE . . . HIRING OUTSIDE HELP.

I'M HOPING THE REST OF THE SCHOOL YEAR WILL YIELD RESULTS MORE PROMISING THAN LAST YEAR. I CAN'T IMAGINE STAYING AT THIS SCHOOL FOR MUCH LONGER.

SCIENCE 101—LAB SYLLABUS
DR. THADDEUS B. SIVANA

If you are here to study the periodic table, do frog dissections, and discuss proven theories . . . then you are in the wrong class.

I shall expand your minds with the possibilities of all that is out there yet to be discovered and attempted. Only then can you become the mad scientist your dark desires have dreamt of.

- Create black holes
- Discover new uses for antimatter
- Absolve gravity
- Pioneer alternate dimensional time travel
- Unfold trans-warp technology
- Blot out the sun

GREETINGS, FUTURE SCIENTISTS OR LAB DISASTERS! I AM DR. SIVANA.
NOT EVERYONE WILL SURVIVE THIS CLASS. BUT THOSE THAT DO WILL BECOME THE GREAT MAD SCIENTISTS OF TOMORROW.
THOSE THAT DON'T . . . WELL . . .
YOU SHOULD ALL STRIVE TO BE THE BEST, LIKE LEX HERE.
HE SURVIVED A LAB EXPLOSION THAT TOOK AWAY HIS HAIR. IT TRANSFORMED HIM INTO A GREAT SCIENTIST.
FIRST ORDER OF BUSINESS IS YOU MUST DRESS THE PART.
EVERYONE GETS A WHITE LAB COAT AND DARK GLOVES.
YOU MUST ALSO BE ASSIGNED A PARTNER.
IT IS UP TO YOU TO DECIDE WHO WILL BE THE SCIENTIST AND WHO IS ONLY THE HENCHMAN—OR HENCHWOMAN, AS THE CASE MAY BE.

YOU'VE GOT TO BE KIDDING.
THIS IS AWKWARD.
BUT SCIENCE IS AWKWARD. AND RIGHT . . . ALWAYS RIGHT.
HEY, LEX, I ALSO VOTED FOR YOU.

CAREER FAIR

Undecided about your future?
Unsure whether to rule the world or rule the galaxy?

This event is for you!
Learn about all kinds of different jobs! See the special clothes and uniforms they wear, participate in demonstrations, activities, and more!

Plus, free food and the chance to win great prizes!!

DATE: January 30
TIME: 1:00–3:00 p.m.
LOCATION: Ducard Auditorium

DATE: JANUARY 14
FROM: BWAYNE
TO: SMALLVILLE_KID, DIANA_WW41
SUBJECT: CAREER FAIR

A NEW FLYER HAS CAUGHT MY ATTENTION. NOW THAT WE'RE ACTIVE AGAIN, I THINK OUR NEW MISSION SHOULD BE TO ATTEND THE CAREER FAIR AT SCHOOL. LOOK FOR ANYTHING SUSPICIOUS. AND TRY TO SPOT THE PRINCIPAL.

—B

THERE'S A LOT HERE!
SPLIT UP AND REPORT BACK. WE'LL COVER MORE GROUND THAT WAY.
YOU SHOULD BE LOCKED UP!
EXCUSE ME?
WITH A JOB AT ARKHAM ASYLUM, YOU CAN WORK BEHIND BARS TO KEEP OUR PATIENTS SECURE.
ARKHAM
NO THANKS.
WE'LL BE KEEPING AN EYE ON YOU, MR. WAYNE!
M.E.A.N.
EVIL CORP.

DO YOU LIKE WHAT YOU SEE?
IT LOOKS INTRIGUING.
I'D BE INTERESTED IN FINDING OUT MORE INFORMATION.
BUT WE'RE NOT INTERESTED IN YOU.
SO DON'T BOTHER!
IS THIS THE BOY YOU TOLD ME ABOUT, LEX?

DATE: FEBRUARY 1

USERNAME: BWAYNE

RE: JOURNAL ENTRY 17

THIS “EVIL” CAREER FAIR DIDN’T PAN OUT TO BE ANYTHING. IT FEATURED A LOT OF QUESTIONABLE COMPANIES LOOKING FOR STUDENTS TO SHAPE TO THEIR OWN BENEFIT. MOST SEEMED TO HAVE WEIRD OPERATIONS RUNNING ON PRIVATE ISLANDS OR ABANDONED MILITARY COMPOUNDS. THE ONLY ONE THAT SHOWED ANY INTEREST IN ME WAS THE ARKHAM FACILITY. I’LL HAVE TO REMEMBER TO FIND OUT MORE ABOUT THEM.

AND IT WAS NO SURPRISE THAT THE PRINCIPAL WAS NOWHERE TO BE FOUND. HOW DO YOU EVEN RUN A SCHOOL IF YOU NEVER APPEAR AT THEIR FUNCTIONS?

HEE-HEE
MREOW HAPPY VALENTINE'S DAY, BRUCE.

Be my Valentine right meow!
- Selina
Takin' you my target!
- Talia

be mine!
-Zatanna
you make my heart sing!
don't leaf me hangin'!
Ivy
My heart skips a beat for you!
-Bekka!

DATE: FEBRUARY 18

USERNAME: BWAYNE

RE: JOURNAL ENTRY 18

I HAVE DECIDED TO TAKE MATTERS INTO MY OWN HANDS, BUT I NEED A COMPUTER TO DO IT. ALFRED CONTINUES TO TAKE AWAY MY INTERNET PRIVILEGES AT HOME FOR ANY NUMBER OF OFFENSES. THIS TIME IT WAS FOR USING HIS PHONE TO ORDER PIZZA. HE SEEMS TO THINK TWENTY OF THEM IS A LOT AND A PUNISHABLE OFFENSE. BUT I WAS HUNGRY!

WITHOUT ACCESS TO MY HOME COMPUTER AND DENIED ACCESS THROUGH THE SCHOOL, I HAVE DECIDED TO TURN TO AN OUTSIDE CONSULTANT TO HELP ME WITH MY SEARCH FOR "NANDA PARBAT." A PRIVATE INVESTIGATION AGENCY I'M PAYING FOR OUT OF MY BIRTHDAY AND HOLIDAY ALLOWANCE.

I AWAIT THEIR RESPONSE.

"If you're looking for an answer, then we've got the Question."

February 25

Wayne Manor of Gotham City
c/o Bruce Wayne
Re: Nanda Parbat

Dear Bruce,

I was able to uncover the answer to your inquiry about the name Nanda Parbat, but it wasn't easy. Not through normal records and background checks. More from anonymous sources and conspiracy channels off the beaten path. So without further ado . . .

Nanda Parbat is a fabled hidden city located in the mountains of Tibet. Its exact location and purpose is unknown. But it dates back many centuries.

I realize it's not much, but at least it's something. May the information be put to good use.

Sincerely,

VIC

Vic Sage, PI

NOW, I WONDER WHY A PLACE IN TIBET NEEDS STUDENTS?
I *KNEW* THERE WERE NINJA HERE. I *KNEW* IT!

DUCARD ACADEMY

Mister Pennyworth

We regret to inform you that you're needed to pick up Bruce early from school.

There's been some trouble.

Check in at the front desk of the office at your earliest convenience.

EXCUSE ME, MA'AM. I'M HERE FOR THE TROUBLEMAKER.
THEY'RE ALL TROUBLE. CAN YOU BE MORE SPECIFIC?
BRUCE—
OUR FAVORITE. OVER THERE, AGAINST THE WALL.

MY WORD!
YOU SHOULD SEE HOW THEY LOOK.
I DID NOT TEACH YOU TO FIGHT BULLIES, YOUNG SIR!
NINJA SELF-DEFENSE.
NINJA . . . MANIACAL CLOWNS . . . SECRET SOCIETIES.
I CERTAINLY WON'T BE A WILLING PARTNER IN YOUR FLIGHTS OF FANCY, SIR!

DATE: March 2
FROM: BWAYNE
TO: SMALLVILLE_KID, DIANA_WW41
SUBJECT: Suspension

I'VE BEEN SUSPENDED FROM SCHOOL FOR THE WEEK. THIS IS WHAT HAPPENS WHEN YOU GET TOO CLOSE TO THE TRUTH. THAT, AND NINJA JUMP YOU (YES, I'M SERIOUS . . . NINJA!!!)

IT'S UP TO YOU BOTH TO KEEP INVESTIGATING THE SCHOOL WHILE I'M AWAY. THEN FILL ME IN ON WHAT YOU FIND.

—B

GLAD TO FINALLY MEET WITH YOU, MR. PRESIDENT.
YES, PRINCIPAL—
SHH! THERE'S NO NEED FOR THAT.
I'VE DECIDED TO SHIFT MY PRIORITIES INTO "REEDUCATION" TOWARD SOME STUDENTS THAT AREN'T WITH THE PROGRAM.
WE'VE BEEN SAVING THIS FOR A SPECIAL OCCASION. THIS MIGHT HELP.
PLACE THIS LEAD BOX SOMEWHERE CLARK KENT WON'T EXPECT IT.
CAN YOU DO THAT FOR ME?
AGAINST MY ONETIME CAMPAIGN RIVAL? ABSOLUTELY!
GASP!
KRYPTONITE . . .

MESSAGES

GROUP CHAT

Msg failed to send

SEND

KRAK!
POW!
LET GO!
KRAK!

DATE: MARCH 10

USERNAME: BWAYNE

RE: JOURNAL ENTRY 19

I'VE BEEN HOME, SUSPENDED FROM SCHOOL FOR THE PAST WEEK. NOW MY FIRST DAY BACK AND SOMETHING HAS HAPPENED TO CLARK AND DIANA. THEY'RE MISSING. THEY AREN'T ANSWERING THEIR TEXTS OR EMAILS. I'M FEARING THE WORST.

WHAT I WON'T DO IS PANIC OR QUIT. I'M SURE THOSE RESPONSIBLE EXPECT AND WANT THAT TO HAPPEN. I WON'T GIVE THEM THAT SATISFACTION.

NOW MORE THAN EVER, I NEED TO BECOME THE GREATEST INVESTIGATOR . . . THE GREATEST DETECTIVE I CAN BE.

CLARK?! DIANA?!
THEY'RE MORE DANGEROUS THAN I POSSIBLY IMAGINED! NO WONDER DUCARD WAS INTERESTED.
CLARK, DIANA! WHAT HAPPENED TO YOU? THIS ISN'T YOU. WHO DID THIS?

QUIT IT, CLARK! MORNING TRASH IS THE WORST!
WAS THAT PANCAKE SYRUP? *GROSS!!* STOP IT, DIANA!
I CAN'T TALK ANY SENSE INTO THEM. BETTER TO GET AWAY BEFORE THEY DO WORSE.
IT'S BAD ENOUGH WHEN BANE TRASHES ME. I DON'T WANT MY FRIENDS TO DO IT TO ME, TOO!

DATE: MARCH 16

USERNAME: BWAYNE

RE: JOURNAL ENTRY 20

CLARK AND DIANA HAVE CHANGED AND IT'S NOT GOOD. UNTIL I'M ABLE TO DISCOVER WHO AND WHAT DID THIS, AND HOW TO REVERSE IT . . . I NEED TO HIDE.

TRYING TO EVADE MY FRIENDS IS ONE OF THE HARDEST THINGS I'VE HAD TO DO. I'VE MANAGED TO STAY OUT OF SIGHT USING THE VENTILATION SHAFTS TO MOVE AROUND CAMPUS. I SWEAR I HEARD CLARK SAY HE CAN SEE THROUGH WALLS. BUT SOMEHOW HE ISN'T ABLE TO SEE THROUGH A SIMPLE LEAD-LINED SHAFT.

WITH THE INCREASED NINJA PATROLS, IT'S ONLY A MATTER OF TIME BEFORE I GET CAUGHT. SO I HAVE TO THINK FAST, WEAR MY BATMAN COSTUME DISGUISE, AND GO FIND CLUES, STARTING WITH MY FRIENDS' LOCKERS. SEE IF THERE'S ANYTHING THERE THAT CAN HELP ME.

HOW NOT TO CAPTURE YOUR FRIENDS:

Only use this
when you want
to find out
the truth!

HALLWAY-MONITOR 02
11:22:14
HALLWAY-MONITOR 03
11:31:16
HALLWAY-MONITOR 01
11:35:12

DATE: MARCH 17

USERNAME: BWAYNE

RE: JOURNAL ENTRY 21

CAPTURING MY FRIENDS PROVED TO BE TOUGH. BUT I MANAGED TO GET THEM DOWN TO THE BASEMENT TO QUESTION THEM. DIANA'S LASSO FROM HER LOCKER ACTUALLY HAS SPECIAL PROPERTIES. SOME MIGHT SAY MAGIC. BUT DEFINITELY HELPS GET TO THE TRUTH.

THEY TELL ME THAT DR. SIVANA CREATED A HELMET ALONG WITH TECHNOLOGY FROM MR. TETCH TO MAKE THE USER THAT WEARS IT SUSCEPTIBLE TO COMMANDS. A BRAINWASH DEVICE! TALIA WAS ALSO AN ACCOMPLICE. BUT THEY DON'T KNOW IF THE PRINCIPAL IS IN CHARGE.

THIS ROPE COULD DEFINITELY COME IN HANDY LATER. ALFRED WOULD NEVER BE ABLE TO HIDE SNACKS FROM ME IN THE HOUSE EVER AGAIN.

Mad science
Mad hat
Mad
science
HAT

LET'S GET THAT HELMET.
LET'S DESTROY THAT HELMET!
BUT FIRST, LET'S CHANGE INTO SOMETHING MORE . . . HEROIC!

POW!
WOK!
I ALWAYS HATED SCIENCE . . . *MAD SCIENCE.*
ALICE, HOW COULD YOU?
MY NAME IS DIANA!
NICE TRY. BUT I'M NOT ALONE.
NEITHER AM I.

WHO IS RESPONSIBLE FOR THIS SCHOOL, TALIA? FOR EVERYTHING HERE?
I CAN ANSWER. THAT WOULD BE ME.
I AM YOUR PRINCIPAL. HER FATHER. AND MY NAME IS **RĀ'S AL GHŪL!**

WHO?
I JUST WANT TO KNOW ONE THING . . . WHY?
I AM THE MASTER OF SHADOWS. THE DEMON'S HEAD. THE . . .
NEVER MIND.
I TOOK OVER THIS SCHOOL TO FIND AND TRAIN NEW MEMBERS FOR MY ORGANIZATION, THE LEAGUE OF ASSASSINS. WITH OUR SOCIETY CRUMBLING, OUR JOB IS TO REBUILD WITH THE VERY BEST . . . MY STUDENTS. WE'VE DONE IT FOR CENTURIES.
HISTORY CLASS . . . OF COURSE! IT WAS EXPLAINED IN OUR BOOKS WHAT YOU'VE DONE THROUGHOUT TIME.
EVEN THE SCHOOL GROUNDS WERE A HINT. ANCIENT SCULPTURES AND STATUES EVERYWHERE FROM MULTIPLE DYNASTIES AND EMPIRES YOU'VE HELPED CONQUER.

IT'S A SHAME REALLY. WE HELPED MOLD SO MANY YOUNG MINDS, DIDN'T WE, MY DAUGHTER.
YES, FATHER.
BUT NOT EVERYONE TOOK TO THEIR EDUCATION.
YES, WE DID. YOU TAUGHT US THAT ALL EMPIRES MUST FALL. INCLUDING YOURS.
WHICH IS WHY THE CASE I'VE—THAT ***WE'VE*** BEEN BUILDING, HAS BEEN SHARED WITH THE GOTHAM CITY POLICE DEPARTMENT.
THAT SHOULD BE THEM RIGHT NOW.

TOO BAD WE WON'T BE AROUND TO GREET THEM.
WELL PLAYED, JUNIOR DETECTIVE.
THAT'S "WORLD'S GREATEST DETECTIVE" TO YOU. **AND NOT JUNIOR!!**
ONE DAY I'LL HAVE A JET, TOO.
I HAVE A JET!
I'LL BELIEVE IT WHEN I SEE IT. BUT THANKS.

Hi Bruce,

What a wild year it's been! While I'm happy to be home, I miss you and Clark. I hope to see you soon. Until then, use your detective skills and see if you can spot my Invisible Jet on this postcard. I parked it near the beach.

- Diana

P.S. It's there . . . you just have to look! :)

BRUCE WAYNE
WAYNE MANOR
GOTHAM CITY

DATE: MARCH 30

USERNAME: BWAYNE

RE: JOURNAL ENTRY 22

IT'S BEEN A COUPLE OF WEEKS SINCE THE DUCARD ACADEMY SHUT DOWN FOR GOOD DUE TO OUR INVESTIGATION. THE SCHOOL HAS EVEN BEEN REOPENED WITH PROPER EDUCATORS. WHILE RĀ'S AL GHŪL AND HIS DAUGHTER HAVE ESCAPED, AND I HAVE NO MEANS TO TRAVEL AND FIND NANDA PARBAT, I WILL INSTEAD WAIT VIGILANTLY. IF THEY EVER COME BACK, I'LL BE READY FOR THEM. THE TEACHERS INVOLVED IN THE SCANDAL WERE ALL GIVEN COMMUNITY SERVICE AND THE STUDENTS WILL BE SENT TO SUMMER SCHOOL. I THINK THE GOOD GUYS WON THIS TIME.

CASE CLOSED.

I BECAME A LATE TRANSFER TO A SMALL PUBLIC SCHOOL. ONE WHERE NOTHING WEIRD EVER HAPPENS. ONE WITHOUT NINJA OR CLOWNS. EVEN THE CAFETERIA FOOD IS UNINSPIRING. BUT IT BEATS THE ALTERNATIVE.

I STILL KEEP IN CONTACT WITH MY FRIENDS. CLARK WENT BACK TO SMALLVILLE. HE'LL BE HOME TUTORED UNTIL HE CAN START THE NEXT GRADE. DIANA IS LIVING BACK WITH HER MOTHER AND SISTERS ON PARADISE ISLAND. THAT'S GOTTA BE NICE!

ALFRED THINKS I SHOULD GIVE CAMP A TRY. HE SAYS IT'S DARK IN THE FOREST. CREEPY. WITH LOTS OF BATS. AND I'M SURE A MYSTERY OR TWO TO SOLVE.

IF THERE'S ONE THING I'VE LEARNED, IT'S THAT ALFRED ALWAYS KNOWS WHAT'S BEST FOR ME.

Case File
Folder of Rā's
[SOLVED]

Derek Fridolfs

works in the comic industry as a writer, inker, and artist on many beloved properties. With Dustin Nguyen, he co-wrote *Batman: Li'l Gotham* and *Justice League Beyond*. He's also written for such titles as *Batman: Arkham City Endgame, Arkham Unhinged, Detective Comics, Legends of the Dark Knight, Adventures of Superman, Sensation Comics Featuring Wonder Woman, Catwoman, Zatanna, JLA,* and comics based on the cartoons for *Adventure Time, Regular Show, Dexter's Laboratory, Looney Tunes,* and *Teenage Mutant Ninja Turtles.*

Derek enjoys traveling, late-night movie watching, book shopping, and just about all pizza.

This is his first children's book, and he looks forward to many more.

Dustin Nguyen

is best known for his many interpretations of Batman for DC Comics, including the co-creation of DC's all-ages series *Batman: Li'l Gotham,* written by himself and Derek Fridolfs. Currently, he illustrates lots and lots of robots and aliens on *Descender*, a monthly comic published through Image Comics, of which he is also co-creator, alongside artist/writer Jeff Lemire. Outside of comics, Dustin also moonlights as a conceptual artist for toys and consumer products, games, and animation. He enjoys sleeping, driving, and sketching things he cares about.